53rd Annual Meeting of the Association for Computational Linguistics and 7th International Joint Conference on Natural Language Processing of the Asian Federation of Natural Language Processing

(ACL-IJCNLP 2015)

Student Research Workshop

Beijing, China
26 – 31 July 2015

ISBN: 978-1-5108-0848-5

Printed from e-media with permission by:

Curran Associates, Inc.
57 Morehouse Lane
Red Hook, NY 12571

Some format issues inherent in the e-media version may also appear in this print version.

Printed by Curran Associates, Inc. (2015)

For permission requests, please contact the Association for Computational Linguistics
at the address below.

Association for Computational Linguistics
209 N. Eighth Street
Stroudsburg, Pennsylvania 18360

Phone: 1-570-476-8006
Fax: 1-570-476-0860

acl@aclweb.org

Additional copies of this publication are available from:

Curran Associates, Inc.
57 Morehouse Lane
Red Hook, NY 12571 USA
Phone: 845-758-0400
Fax: 845-758-2634
Email: curran@proceedings.com
Web: www.proceedings.com

ACL-IJCNLP 2015

The 53rd Annual Meeting of the Association for Computational Linguistics and the 7th International Joint Conference on Natural Language Processing

Proceedings of the Student Research Workshop

July 28, 2015
Beijing, China

Introduction

Welcome to the ACJ-IJCNLP 2015 Student Research Workshop!

Following the tradition of the previous years' workshops, we have two tracks: research papers and thesis proposals. The research papers track is as a venue for Ph.D. students, masters students, and advanced undergraduates to describe completed work or work-in-progress along with preliminary results. The thesis proposal track is offered for advanced Ph.D. students who have decided on a thesis topic and are interested in feedback about their proposal and ideas about future directions for their work.

We received in total 18 submissions: 5 thesis proposals and 13 research papers. Of these, we accepted 3 thesis proposals and 4 research papers, giving an acceptance rate of 39% overall: 60% for thesis proposals and 31% for research papers.

This year, all of the accepted papers will be presented as posters alongside the main conference short paper posters on the second day of the conference. In addition, authors will each have a chance to give a short oral presentation to advertise their work. The oral session will be held on immediately prior to the poster session.

Mentoring programs are a central part of the SRW. This year, students had the opportunity to participate in a pre-submission mentoring program prior to the submission deadline. The mentoring offers students a chance to receive comments from an experienced researcher in the field, in order to improve the quality of the writing and presentation before making their final submission. Fourteen authors participated in the pre-submission mentoring, more than twice as many as participated last year.

In addition, authors of accepted papers are matched with mentors who will meet with the students in person during the workshop. This year, each research paper is assigned two mentors and each thesis proposal is assigned one mentor. Each mentor will prepare in-depth comments and questions prior to the student's presentation, and will provide discussion and feedback during the workshop.

We are very grateful for the generous financial support from BAOBAG Language Solutions, Google, the Don and Betty Walker Scholarship Fund, and the National Science Foundation. The support of our sponsors allows the SRW to cover the travel and lodging expenses of the authors, keeping the workshop accessible to all students.

We would also like to thank our program committee members for their constructive reviews for each paper and all of our mentors for donating their time to work one-on-one with our student authors. Thank you to our faculty advisers for their advice and guidance, and to the ACL-IJCNLP 2015 organizing committee for their constant support. Finally, a huge thank you to all students for their submissions and their participation in this year's SRW. Looking forward to a wonderful workshop!

Organizers:

Kuan-Yu Chen, National Taiwan University
Angelina Ivanova, University of Oslo
Ellie Pavlick, University of Pennsylvania

Faculty Advisors:

Emily Bender, University of Washington
Chin-Yew Lin, Microsoft
Stephan Oepen, University of Oslo

Program Committee:

Timothy Baldwin, University of Melbourne
Srinivas Bangalore, AT&T Labs-Research
António Branco, University of Lisbon
Chris Brew, Thomson-Reuters
Claire Cardie, Cornell University
John Carroll, University of Sussex
Stephen Clark, University of Cambridge
Walter Daelemans, University of Antwerp
Michael Elhadad, Ben-Gurion University of the Negev
Katrin Erk, University of Texas at Austin
George Foster, Google
Ralph Grishman, New York University
Jan Hajič, Charles University in Prague
Dilek Hakkani-Tur, Microsoft Research
Lars Hellan, Norwegian University of Science and Technology
Kristiina Jokinen, University of Helsinki
Aravind K. Joshi, University of Pennsylvania
Min-Yen Kan, National University of Singapore
Kevin Knight, University of Southern California
Philipp Koehn, University of Edinburgh
Sadao Kurohashi, Kyoto University
Zheng-Hua Li, Soochow University
Wei Lu, Singapore University of Technology and Design
Daniel Marcu, University of Southern California
Mitchell Marcus, University of Pennsylvania
Diana McCarthy, University of Cambridge
Kathy McKeown, Columbia University
Rada Mihalcea, University of Michigan
Alessandro Moschitti, University of Trento
Vincent Ng, The University of Texas at Dallas
Joakim Nivre, Uppsala University
Kemal Oflazer, Carnegie Mellon University in Qatar
Miles Osborne, Bloomberg

Massimo Poesio, University of Essex
Jonathon Read, Teesside University
Satoshi Sekine, New York University
Mark Steedman, University of Edinburgh
Keh-Yih Su, National Tsing Hua University
Mihai Surdeanu, Univesity of Arizona

Pre-submission Mentors:

Marine Carpuat, National Research Council Canada
Silvie Cinková, Charles University in Prague
Hal Daumé III, University of Maryland
Michael Gamon, Microsoft Research
Ralph Grishman, New York University
Sophia Katrenko, Elsevier
Haizhou Li, Institute for Infocomm Research
Yang Liu, University of Texas at Dallas
Adam Lopez, Johns Hopkins University
Mei Ling Meng, Chinese University of Hong Kong
Petya Osenova, Sofia University
Philip Resnik, University of Maryland
Jörg Tiedemann, Uppsala University
Rui Wang, Trendiction S.A.
Bonnie Webber, University of Edinburgh
Yi Zhang, Nuance Communications

Mentors for Accepted Papers:

Francis Bond, Nanyang Technological University
Wanxiang Che, Harbin Institute of Technology
Wenliang Chen, Soochow University
Graeme Hirst, University of Toronto
Dirk Hovy, University of Copenhagen
Ndapandula Nakashole, Carnegie Mellon University
Alan Ritter, Carnegie Mellon University
Jon Scott Stevens, Zentrum für Allgemeine Sprachwissenschaft
Wei Xu, University of Pennsylvania
Nianwen Xue, Brandeis University
Yue Zhang, Singapore University of Technology and Design

Table of Contents

Workshop Program

Monday, July 27, 2015

11:50–13:20 ***Student Lunch***

Tuesday, July 28, 2015

16:30–17:55 ***Student Oral Presentations***

18:00–19:30 ***Poster and Dinner Session***

Unsupervised Learning and Modeling of Knowledge and Intent for Spoken Dialogue Systems

Yun-Nung Chen
School of Computer Science, Carnegie Mellon University
5000 Forbes Avenue, Pittsburgh, PA 15213-3891, USA
yvchen@cs.cmu.edu

Abstract

Spoken dialogue systems (SDS) are rapidly appearing in various smart devices (smartphone, smart-TV, in-car navigating system, etc). The key role in a successful SDS is a spoken language understanding (SLU) component, which parses user utterances into semantic concepts in order to understand users' intentions. However, such semantic concepts and their structure are manually created by experts, and the annotation process results in extremely high cost and poor scalability in system development. Therefore, the dissertation focuses on improving SDS generalization and scalability by automatically inferring domain knowledge and learning structures from unlabeled conversations through a matrix factorization (MF) technique. With the automatically acquired semantic concepts and structures, we further investigate whether such information can be utilized to effectively understand user utterances and then show the feasibility of reducing human effort during SDS development.

1 Introduction

Various smart devices (e.g. smartphone, smart-TV, in-car navigating system) are incorporating spoken language interfaces, a.k.a. spoken dialogue systems (SDS), in order to help users finish tasks more efficiently. The key role in a successful SDS is a spoken language understanding (SLU) component; in order to capture the language variation from dialogue participants, the SLU component must create a mapping between the natural language inputs and semantic representations that correspond to users' intentions.

The semantic representation must include "concepts' and a "structure": concepts are the domain-specific topics, and the structure describes the relations between concepts and conveys intentions. However, most prior work focused on learning the mapping between utterances and semantic representations, where such knowledge still remains predefined. The need of annotations results in extremely high cost and poor scalability in system development. Therefore, current technology usually limits conversational interactions to a few narrow predefined domains/topics. With the increasing conversational interactions, this dissertation focuses on improving *generalization* and *scalability* of building SDSs with little human effort.

In order to achieve the goal, two questions need to be addressed: 1) Given unlabelled conversations, how can a system automatically induce and organize the domain-specific concepts? 2) With the automatically acquired knowledge, how can a system understand user utterances and intents? To tackle the above problems, we propose to acquire the domain knowledge that captures human's semantics, intents, and behaviors. Then based on the acquired knowledge, we build an SLU component to understand users and to offer better interactions in dialogues.

The dissertation shows the feasibility of building a dialogue learning system that is able to understand how particular domains work based on unlabeled conversations. As a result, an initial SDS can be automatically built according to the learned knowledge, and its performance can be quickly improved by interacting with users for practical usage, presenting the potential of reducing human effort for SDS development.

2 Related Work

Unsupervised SLU Tur et al. (2011; 2012) were among the first to consider unsupervised approaches for SLU, where they exploited query logs for slot-filling. In a subsequent study, Heck and Hakkani-Tür (2012) studied the Semantic Web for

Proceedings of the ACL-IJCNLP 2015 Student Research Workshop, pages 1–7,
Beijing, China, July 28, 2015.

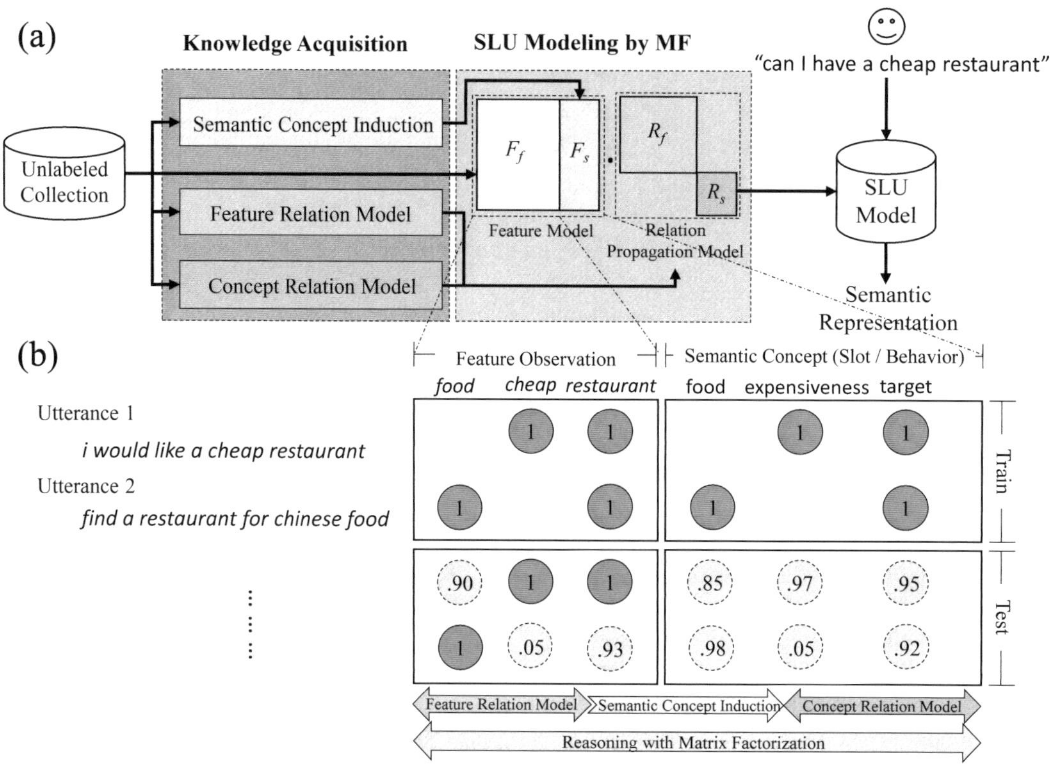

Figure 1: (a): The proposed framework. (b): Our MF method completes a partially-missing matrix for semantic decoding/behavior prediction. Dark circles are observed facts, shaded circles are inferred facts. The ontology induction maps observed feature patterns to semantic concepts. The feature relation model constructs correlations between observed feature patterns. The concept relation model learns the high-level semantic correlations for inferring hidden semantic slots or predicting subsequent behaviors. Reasoning with matrix factorization incorporates these models jointly, and produces a coherent and domain-specific SLU model.

the intent detection problem in SLU, showing that results obtained from the unsupervised training process align well with the performance of traditional supervised learning. Following their success of unsupervised SLU, recent studies have also obtained interesting results on the tasks of relation detection (Hakkani-Tür et al., 2013; Chen et al., 2014a), entity extraction (Wang et al., 2014), and extending domain coverage (El-Kahky et al., 2014; Chen and Rudnicky, 2014). However, most studies above do not explicitly learn latent factor representations from the data—while we hypothesize that the better robustness can be achieved by explicitly modeling the measurement errors (usually produced by automatic speech recognizers (ASR)) using latent variable models and taking additional local and global semantic constraints into account.

Latent Variable Modeling in SLU Early studies on latent variable modeling in speech included the classic hidden Markov model for statistical speech recognition (Jelinek, 1997). Recently, Celikyilmaz et al. (2011) were the first to study the intent detection problem using query logs and a discrete Bayesian latent variable model. In the field of dialogue modeling, the partially observable Markov decision process (POMDP) (Young et al., 2013) model is a popular technique for dialogue management, reducing the cost of handcrafted dialogue managers while producing robustness against speech recognition errors. More recently, Tur et al. (2013) used a semi-supervised LDA model to show improvement on the slot filling task. Also, Zhai and Williams (2014) proposed an unsupervised model for connecting words with latent states in HMMs using topic models, obtaining interesting qualitative and quantitative results. However, for unsupervised SLU, it is not obvious how to incorporate additional information in the HMMs. With increasing works about learning the feature matrices for language representations (Mikolov et al., 2013), matrix factorization (MF) has become very popular for both implicit and explicit feedback (Rendle et al., 2009; Chen et al., 2015a).

This thesis proposal is the first to propose a framework about unsupervised SLU modeling, which is able to simultaneously consider various local and global knowledge automatically learned from unlabelled data using a matrix factorization (MF) technique.

3 The Proposed Work

The proposed framework is shown in Figure 1(a), where there are two main parts, one is *knowledge acquisition* and another is *SLU modeling by MF*. The first part is to acquire the domain knowledge that is useful for building the domain-specific dialogue systems, which addresses the question about how to induce and organize the semantic concepts (the first problem). Here we propose ontology induction and structure learning procedures. The ontology induction refers to the semantic concept induction (yellow block) and the structure learning refers to relation models (blue and pink blocks) in Figure 1(a). The details are described in Section 4. The second part is to self-train an SLU component using the acquired knowledge for the domain-specific SDS, and this part answers to the question about how to utilize the obtained information in SDSs to understand user utterances and intents. There are two aspects regarding to SLU modeling, semantic decoding and behavior prediction. The semantic decoding is to parse the input utterances into semantic forms for better understanding, and the behavior prediction is to predict the subsequent user behaviors for providing better system interactions. This dissertation plans to apply MF techniques to unsupervised SLU modeling, including both semantic decoding and behavior prediction.

In the proposed model, we first build a feature matrix to represent training utterances, where each row refers to an utterance and each column refers to an observed feature pattern or a learned semantic concept (either a slot or a behavior). Figure 1(b) illustrates an example of the matrix. Then given a testing utterance, we can convert it into a vector based on the observed patterns, and fill in the missing values of the semantic concepts. In the first example utterance of the figure, although semantic slot food is not observed, the utterance implies the meaning facet food. The MF approach is able to learn the latent feature vectors for utterances and semantic concepts, inferring implicit semantics to improve the decoding process—namely, by filling the matrix with probabilities (lower part of the matrix in Figure 1(b)).

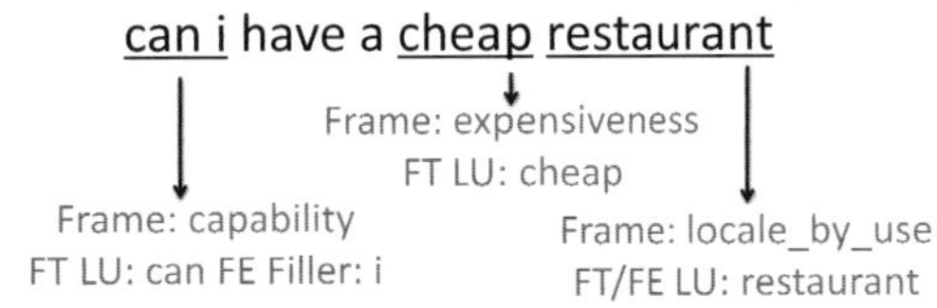

Figure 2: An example of probabilistic frame-semantic parsing on ASR output. FT: frame target. FE: frame element. LU: lexical unit.

The feature model is built on the observed feature patterns and the learned concepts, where the concepts are obtained from the knowledge acquisition process (Chen et al., 2013; Chen et al., 2015b). Section 5.1 explains the detail of the feature model. In order to consider the additional structure information, we propose a relation propagation model based on the learned structure, which includes a feature relation model (blue block) and a concept relation model (pink block) described in Section 5.2.

Finally we train an SLU model by learning latent feature vectors for utterances and slots/behaviors through MF techniques. Combining with a relation propagation model, the trained SLU model is able to estimate the probability that each concept occurs in the testing utterance, and how likely each concept is domain-specific simultaneously. In other words, the SLU model is able to transform testing utterances into domain-specific semantic representations or predicted behaviors without human involvement.

4 Knowledge Acquisition

Given unlabeled conversations and available knowledge resources, we plan to extract organized knowledge that can be used for domain-specific SDSs. The ontology induction and structure learning are proposed to automate an ontology building process.

4.1 Ontology Induction

Chen et al. (2013; 2014b) proposed to automatically induce semantic slots for SDSs by frame-semantic parsing, where all ASR-decoded utter-

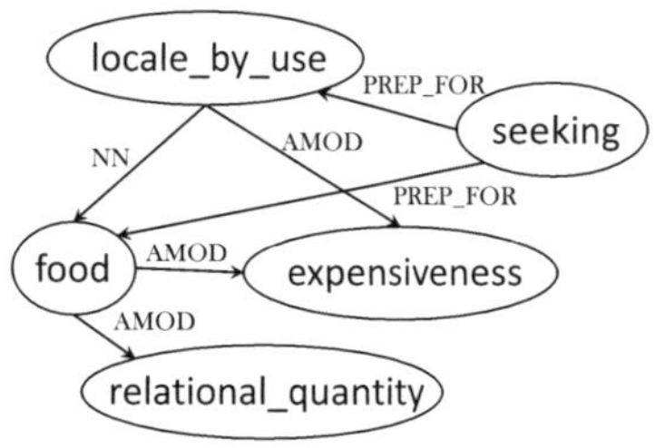

Figure 3: A simplified example of the automatically derived knowledge graph.

ances are parsed using SEMAFOR[1], a state-of-the-art frame-semantic parser (Das et al., 2010; Das et al., 2013), and then all frames from parsed results are extracted as slot candidates (Dinarelli et al., 2009). For example, Figure 2 shows an example of an ASR-decoded text output parsed by SEMAFOR. There are three frames (capability, expensiveness, and locale_by_use) in the utterance, which we consider as slot candidates.

Since SEMAFOR was trained on FrameNet annotation, which has a more generic frame-semantic context, not all the frames from the parsing results can be used as the actual slots in the domain-specific dialogue systems. For instance, in Figure 2, "expensiveness" and "locale_by_use" frames are essentially the key slots for the purpose of understanding in the restaurant query domain, whereas the "capability" frame does not convey particularly valuable information for the domain-specific SDS. In order to fix this issue, Chen et al. (2014b) proved that integrating continuous-valued word embeddings with a probabilistic frame-semantic parser is able to identify key semantic slots in an unsupervised fashion, reducing the cost of designing task-oriented SDSs.

4.2 Structure Learning

A key challenge of designing a coherent semantic ontology for SLU is to consider the structure and relations between semantic concepts. In practice, however, it is difficult for domain experts and professional annotators to define a coherent slot set, while considering various lexical, syntactic, and semantic dependencies. The previous work exploited the typed syntactic dependency theory for unsupervised induction and organization of semantic slots in SDSs (Chen et al., 2015b). More specifically, two knowledge graphs, a slot-based semantic knowledge graph and a word-based lexical knowledge graph, are automatically constructed. To jointly consider the word-to-word, word-to-slot, and slot-to-slot relations, we use a random walk inference algorithm to combine these two knowledge graphs, guided by dependency grammars. Figure 3 is a simplified example of the automatically built semantic knowledge graph corresponding to the restaurant domain. The experiments showed that considering inter-slot relations is crucial for generating a more coherent and compete slot set, resulting in a better SLU model, while enhancing the interpretability of semantic slots.

[1] http://www.ark.cs.cmu.edu/SEMAFOR/

5 SLU Modeling by Matrix Factorization

For two aspects of SLU modeling: semantic decoding and behavior prediction, we plan to apply MF to both tasks by treating learned concepts as semantic slots and human behaviors respectively.

Considering the benefits brought by MF techniques, including 1) modeling the noisy data, 2) modeling hidden information, and 3) modeling the dependency between observations, the dissertation applies an MF approach to SLU modeling for SDSs. In our model, we use U to denote the set of input utterances, F as the set of observed feature patterns, and S as the set of semantic concepts we would like to predict (slots or human behaviors). The pair of an utterance $u \in U$ and a feature/concept $x \in \{F + S\}$, $\langle u, x \rangle$, is a *fact*. The input to our model is a set of observed facts $\mathcal{O}$, and the observed facts for a given utterance is denoted by $\{\langle u, x \rangle \in \mathcal{O}\}$. The goal of our model is to estimate, for a given utterance u and a given feature pattern/concept x, the probability, $p(M_{u,x} = 1)$, where $M_{u,x}$ is a binary random variable that is true if and only if x is the feature pattern/domain-specific concept in the utterance u. We introduce a series of exponential family models that estimate the probability using a natural parameter $\theta_{u,x}$ and the logistic sigmoid function:

$$\begin{aligned} p(M_{u,x} = 1 \mid \theta_{u,x}) &= \sigma(\theta_{u,x}) \\ &= \frac{1}{1 + \exp(-\theta_{u,x})}. \end{aligned} \tag{1}$$

We construct a matrix $M_{|U| \times (|F| + |S|)}$ as observed facts for MF by integrating a feature model and a relation propagation model below.

5.1 Feature Model

First, we build a binary feature pattern matrix F_f based on the observations, where each row refers to an utterance and each column refers to a feature pattern (a word or a phrase). In other words, F_f carries the basic word/phrase vector for each utterance, which is illustrated as the left part of the matrix in Figure 1(b). Then we build a binary matrix F_s based on the induced semantic concepts from Section 4.1, which also denotes the slot/behavior features for all utterances (right part of the matrix in Figure 1(b)).

For building the feature model M_F, we concatenate two matrices and obtain $M_F = [\ F_f \quad F_s\ ]$, which refers to the upper part of the matrix in Figure 1(b) for training utterances.

5.2 Relation Propagation Model

It is shown that the structure of semantic concepts helps decide domain-specific slots and further improves the SLU performance (Chen et al., 2015b). With the learned structure from Section 4.2, we can model the relations between semantic concepts, such as inter-slot and inter-behavior relations. Also, the relations between feature patterns can be modeled in the similar way. We construct two knowledge graphs to model the structure:

- **Feature knowledge graph** is built as $G_f = \langle V_f, E_{ff} \rangle$, where $V_f = \{f_i \in F\}$ and $E_{ff} = \{e_{ij} \mid f_i, f_j \in V_f\}$.
- **Semantic concept knowledge graph** is built as $G_s = \langle V_s, E_{ss} \rangle$, where $V_s = \{s_i \in S\}$ and $E_{ss} = \{e_{ij} \mid s_i, s_j \in V_s\}$.

The structured graph can model the relation between the connected node pair (x_i, x_j) as $r(x_i, x_j)$. Here we compute two matrices $R_s = [r(s_i, s_j)]_{|S|\times|S|}$ and $R_f = [r(f_i, f_j)]_{|F|\times|F|}$ to represent concept relations and feature relations respectively. With the built relation models, we combine them as a relation propagation matrix M_R[2] :

$$M_R = \begin{bmatrix} R_f & 0 \\ 0 & R_s \end{bmatrix}. \quad (2)$$

The goal of this matrix is to propagate scores between nodes according to different types of relations in the constructed knowledge graphs (Chen and Metze, 2012).

5.3 Integrated Model

With a feature model M_F and a relation propagation model M_R, we integrate them into a single matrix.

$$\begin{aligned} M &= M_F \cdot (M_R + I) \quad (3) \\ &= \begin{bmatrix} F_f R_f + F_f & 0 \\ 0 & F_s R_s + F_s \end{bmatrix}, \end{aligned}$$

where M is final matrix and I is the identity matrix in order to remain the original values. The matrix M is similar to M_F, but some weights are enhanced through the relation propagation model. The feature relations are built by $F_f R_f$, which is the matrix with internal weight propagation on the feature knowledge graph (the blue arrow in Figure 1(b)). Similarly, $F_s R_s$ models the semantic concept correlations, and can be treated as the matrix with internal weight propagation on the semantic concept knowledge graph (the pink arrow in Figure 1(b)). The propagation model can be treated as running a random walk algorithm on the graphs.

By integrating with the relation propagation model, the relations can be propagated via the knowledge graphs, and the hidden information may be modeled based on the assumption that mutual relations usually help inference (Chen et al., 2015b). Hence, the structure information can be automatically involved in the matrix. In conclusion, for each utterance, the integrated model not only predicts the probabilities that semantic concepts occur but also considers whether they are domain-specific.

5.4 Model Learning

The proposed model is parameterized through weights and latent component vectors, where the parameters are estimated by maximizing the log likelihood of observed data (Collins et al., 2001).

$$\begin{aligned} \theta^* &= \arg\max_\theta \prod_{u \in U} p(\theta \mid M_u) \quad (4) \\ &= \arg\max_\theta \prod_{u \in U} p(M_u \mid \theta) p(\theta) \\ &= \arg\max_\theta \sum_{u \in U} \ln p(M_u \mid \theta) - \lambda_\theta, \end{aligned}$$

where M_u is the vector corresponding to the utterance u from $M_{u,x}$ in (1), because we assume that each utterance is independent of others.

To avoid treating unobserved facts as designed negative facts, we consider our positive-only data

[2] The values in the diagonal of M_R are 0 to model the propagation from other entries.

as *implicit feedback*. Bayesian Personalized Ranking (BPR) is an optimization criterion that learns from implicit feedback for MF, which uses a variant of the ranking: giving observed true facts higher scores than unobserved (true or false) facts (Rendle et al., 2009). Riedel et al. (2013) also showed that BPR learns the implicit relations and improves a relation extraction task.

To estimate the parameters in (4), we create a dataset of *ranked pairs* from M in (3): for each utterance u and each observed fact $f^+ = \langle u, x^+ \rangle$, where $M_{u,x} \geq \delta$, we choose each semantic concept x^- such that $f^- = \langle u, x^- \rangle$, where $M_{u,x} < \delta$, which refers to the semantic concept we have not observed in utterance u. That is, we construct the observed data $\mathcal{O}$ from M. Then for each pair of facts f^+ and f^-, we want to model $p(f^+) > p(f^-)$ and hence $\theta_{f^+} > \theta_{f^-}$ according to (1). BPR maximizes the summation of each ranked pair, where the objective is

$$\sum_{u \in U} \ln p(M_u \mid \theta) = \sum_{f^+ \in \mathcal{O}} \sum_{f^- \notin \mathcal{O}} \ln \sigma(\theta_{f^+} - \theta_{f^-}). \quad (5)$$

The BPR objective is an approximation to the per utterance AUC (area under the ROC curve), which directly correlates to what we want to achieve – well-ranked semantic concepts per utterance, which denotes the better estimation of semantic slots or human behaviors.

To maximize the objective in (5), we employ a stochastic gradient descent (SGD) algorithm (Rendle et al., 2009). For each randomly sampled observed fact $\langle u, x^+ \rangle$, we sample an unobserved fact $\langle u, x^- \rangle$, which results in $|\mathcal{O}|$ fact pairs $\langle f^-, f^+ \rangle$. For each pair, we perform an SGD update using the gradient of the corresponding objective function for matrix factorization (Gantner et al., 2011).

6 Conclusion and Future Work

This thesis proposal proposes an unsupervised SLU approach by automating the dialogue learning process on speech conversations. The preliminary results show that for the automatic speech recognition (ASR) transcripts (word error rate is about 37%), the acquired knowledge can be successfully applied to SLU modeling through MF techniques, guiding the direction of the methodology.

The main planed tasks include:

- Semantic concept identification
- Semantic concept annotation
- SLU modeling by matrix factorization

In this thesis proposal, ongoing work and future plans have been presented towards an automatically built domain-specific SDS. With increasing semantic resources, such as Google's Knowledge Graph and Microsoft Satori, the dissertation shows the feasibility that utilizing available knowledge improves the generalization and the scalability of dialogue system development for practical usage.

Acknowledgements

I thank my committee members, Prof. Alexander I. Rudnicky, Prof. Anatole Gershman, Prof. Alan W Black, and Dr. Dilek Hakkani-Tür for their advising and anonymous reviewers for their useful comments. I am also grateful to Prof. Mei Ling Meng for her helpful mentoring.

References

Asli Celikyilmaz, Dilek Hakkani-Tür, and Gokhan Tür. 2011. Leveraging web query logs to learn user intent via bayesian discrete latent variable model. In *Proceedings of ICML*.

Yun-Nung Chen and Florian Metze. 2012. Two-layer mutually reinforced random walk for improved multi-party meeting summarization. In *Proceedings of The 4th IEEE Workshop on Spoken Language Tachnology*, pages 461–466.

Yun-Nung Chen and Alexander I. Rudnicky. 2014. Dynamically supporting unexplored domains in conversational interactions by enriching semantics with neural word embeddings. In *Proceedings of 2014 IEEE Spoken Language Technology Workshop (SLT)*, pages 590–595. IEEE.

Yun-Nung Chen, William Yang Wang, and Alexander I Rudnicky. 2013. Unsupervised induction and filling of semantic slots for spoken dialogue systems using frame-semantic parsing. In *Proceedings of 2013 IEEE Workshop on Automatic Speech Recognition and Understanding (ASRU)*, pages 120–125. IEEE.

Yun-Nung Chen, Dilek Hakkani-Tür, and Gokan Tur. 2014a. Deriving local relational surface forms from dependency-based entity embeddings for unsupervised spoken language understanding. In *Proceedings of 2014 IEEE Spoken Language Technology Workshop (SLT)*, pages 242–247. IEEE.

Yun-Nung Chen, William Yang Wang, and Alexander I. Rudnicky. 2014b. Leveraging frame semantics and distributional semantics for unsupervised semantic slot induction in spoken dialogue systems. In *Proceedings of 2014 IEEE Spoken Language Technology Workshop (SLT)*, pages 584–589. IEEE.

Yun-Nung Chen, William Yang Wang, Anatole Gershman, and Alexander I. Rudnicky. 2015a. Matrix factorization with knowledge graph propagation for unsupervised spoken language understanding. In *Proceedings of The 53rd Annual Meeting of the Association for Computational Linguistics and The 7th International Joint Conference on Natural Language Processing of the Asian Federation of Natural Language Processing (ACL-IJCNLP 2015)*. ACL.

Yun-Nung Chen, William Yang Wang, and Alexander I. Rudnicky. 2015b. Jointly modeling inter-slot relations by random walk on knowledge graphs for unsupervised spoken language understanding. In *Proceedings of the 2015 Conference of the North American Chapter of the Association for Computational Linguistics - Human Language Technologies*. ACL.

Michael Collins, Sanjoy Dasgupta, and Robert E Schapire. 2001. A generalization of principal components analysis to the exponential family. In *Proceedings of Advances in Neural Information Processing Systems*, pages 617–624.

Dipanjan Das, Nathan Schneider, Desai Chen, and Noah A Smith. 2010. Probabilistic frame-semantic parsing. In *Proceedings of The Conference of the North American Chapter of the Association for Computational Linguistics: Human Language Technologies*, pages 948–956.

Dipanjan Das, Desai Chen, André F. T. Martins, Nathan Schneider, and Noah A. Smith. 2013. Frame-semantic parsing. *Computational Linguistics*.

Marco Dinarelli, Silvia Quarteroni, Sara Tonelli, Alessandro Moschitti, and Giuseppe Riccardi. 2009. Annotating spoken dialogs: from speech segments to dialog acts and frame semantics. In *Proceedings of the 2nd Workshop on Semantic Representation of Spoken Language*, pages 34–41. ACL.

Ali El-Kahky, Derek Liu, Ruhi Sarikaya, Gökhan Tür, Dilek Hakkani-Tür, and Larry Heck. 2014. Extending domain coverage of language understanding systems via intent transfer between domains using knowledge graphs and search query click logs. In *Proceedings of ICASSP*.

Zeno Gantner, Steffen Rendle, Christoph Freudenthaler, and Lars Schmidt-Thieme. 2011. Mymedialite: A free recommender system library. In *Proceedings of the fifth ACM conference on Recommender systems*, pages 305–308. ACM.

Dilek Hakkani-Tür, Larry Heck, and Gokhan Tur. 2013. Using a knowledge graph and query click logs for unsupervised learning of relation detection. In *Proceedings of ICASSP*, pages 8327–8331.

Larry Heck and Dilek Hakkani-Tür. 2012. Exploiting the semantic web for unsupervised spoken language understanding. In *Proceedings of SLT*, pages 228–233.

Frederick Jelinek. 1997. *Statistical methods for speech recognition*. MIT press.

Tomas Mikolov, Ilya Sutskever, Kai Chen, Greg S Corrado, and Jeff Dean. 2013. Distributed representations of words and phrases and their compositionality. In *Proceedings of Advances in Neural Information Processing Systems*, pages 3111–3119.

Steffen Rendle, Christoph Freudenthaler, Zeno Gantner, and Lars Schmidt-Thieme. 2009. BPR: Bayesian personalized ranking from implicit feedback. In *Proceedings of the Twenty-Fifth Conference on Uncertainty in Artificial Intelligence*, pages 452–461. AUAI Press.

Sebastian Riedel, Limin Yao, Andrew McCallum, and Benjamin M Marlin. 2013. Relation extraction with matrix factorization and universal schemas. In *Proceedings of NAACL-HLT*, pages 74–84.

Gokhan Tur, Dilek Z Hakkani-Tür, Dustin Hillard, and Asli Celikyilmaz. 2011. Towards unsupervised spoken language understanding: Exploiting query click logs for slot filling. In *Proceedings of INTERSPEECH*, pages 1293–1296.

Gokhan Tur, Minwoo Jeong, Ye-Yi Wang, Dilek Hakkani-Tür, and Larry P Heck. 2012. Exploiting the semantic web for unsupervised natural language semantic parsing. In *Proceedings of INTERSPEECH*.

Gokhan Tur, Asli Celikyilmaz, and Dilek Hakkani-Tur. 2013. Latent semantic modeling for slot filling in conversational understanding. In *Proceedings of 2013 IEEE International Conference on Acoustics, Speech and Signal Processing (ICASSP)*, pages 8307–8311. IEEE.

Lu Wang, Dilek Hakkani-Tür, and Larry Heck. 2014. Leveraging semantic web search and browse sessions for multi-turn spoken dialog systems. In *Proceedings of 2014 IEEE International Conference on Acoustics, Speech and Signal Processing (ICASSP)*, pages 4082–4086. IEEE.

Steve Young, Milica Gasic, Blaise Thomson, and Jason D Williams. 2013. POMDP-based statistical spoken dialog systems: A review. *Proceedings of the IEEE*, 101(5):1160–1179.

Ke Zhai and Jason D Williams. 2014. Discovering latent structure in task-oriented dialogues. In *Proceedings of the Association for Computational Linguistics*.

Leveraging Compounds to Improve Noun Phrase Translation from Chinese and German

Xiao Pu
Idiap Research Institute
1920 Martigny
Switzerland
xiao.pu@idiap.ch

Laura Mascarell
Institute of Computational
Linguistics, U. of Zurich
8050 Zurich, Switzerland
mascarell@cl.uzh.ch

Andrei Popescu-Belis
Idiap Research Institute
1920 Martigny
Switzerland
apbelis@idiap.ch

Mark Fishel
Institute of Computational
Linguistics, U. of Zurich
8050 Zurich, Switzerland
fishel@cl.uzh.ch

Ngoc-Quang Luong
Idiap Research Institute
1920 Martigny
Switzerland
nluong@idiap.ch

Martin Volk
Institute of Computational
Linguistics, U. of Zurich
8050 Zurich, Switzerland
volk@cl.uzh.ch

Abstract

This paper presents a method to improve the translation of polysemous nouns, when a previous occurrence of the noun as the head of a compound noun phrase is available in a text. The occurrences are identified through pattern matching rules, which detect XY compounds followed closely by a potentially coreferent occurrence of Y, such as "Nordwand ... Wand". Two strategies are proposed to improve the translation of the second occurrence of Y: re-using the cached translation of Y from the XY compound, or post-editing the translation of Y using the head of the translation of XY. Experiments are performed on Chinese-to-English and German-to-French statistical machine translation, over the WIT3 and Text+Berg corpora respectively, with 261 XY/Y pairs each. The results suggest that while the overall BLEU scores increase only slightly, the translations of the targeted polysemous nouns are significantly improved.

1 Introduction

Words tend to be less ambiguous when considered in context, which partially explains the success of phrase-based statistical machine translation (SMT) systems. In this paper, we take advantage of this observation, and extend the disambiguation potential of n-grams to subsequent occurrences of their individual components. We assume that the translation of a noun-noun compound, noted XY, displays fewer ambiguities than the translations of its components X and Y. Therefore, on a subsequent occurrence of the head of XY, assumed to refer to the same entity as XY, we hypothesize that its previously-found translation offers a better and more coherent translation than the one proposed by an SMT system that is not aware of the compound.

Our claim is supported by results from experiments on Chinese-to-English (ZH/EN) and German-to-French (DE/FR) translation presented in this paper. In both source languages, noun-noun compounds are frequent, and will enable us to disambiguate subsequent occurrences of their head.

For instance, in the example in Figure 1, the Chinese compound 高跟鞋 refers to 'high heels', and the subsequent mention of the referent using only the third character (鞋) should be translated as 'heels'. However, the character 鞋 by itself could also be translated as 'shoe' or 'footwear', as observed with a baseline SMT system that is not aware of the XY/Y coreference.

Although the XY/Y configuration may not be very frequent in texts, errors in its translation are particularly detrimental to the understanding of a text, as they often conceal the coreference link between two expressions. Moreover, as we will show, such issues can be quite reliably corrected, and the proposed approach can later generalize to other configurations of noun phrase coreference.

Proceedings of the ACL-IJCNLP 2015 Student Research Workshop, pages 8–15,
Beijing, China, July 28, 2015.

1. Chinese source sentence	她以为自己买了双两英寸的高跟鞋， 但实际上那是一双三英寸高的鞋。
2. Segmentation, POS tagging, identification of compounds and their co-reference	她#PN 以为#VV 自己#AD 买#VV 了#AS 双#CD 两#CD 英寸#NN 的#DEG 高跟鞋#NN ，#PU 但#AD 实际上#AD 那#PN 是#VC 一#CD 双#M 三#CD 英寸#NN 高#VA 的#DEC 鞋#NN 。#PU
3. Baseline translation into English (statistical MT)	She thought since bought a pair of two inches high heel, but in fact it was a pair of three inches high shoes.
4. Automatic post-editing of the baseline translation using compounds	She thought since bought a pair of two inches high heel, but in fact it was a pair of three inches high heel.
5. Comparison with a human reference translation	She thought she'd gotten a two-inch heel but she'd actually bought a three-inch heel. ✓

Figure 1: Compound post-editing method illustrated on ZH/EN. The first translation of 高跟鞋 into 'heel' enables the correct translation of the subsequent occurrence of 鞋 as 'heel', by post-editing the baseline output 'shoes'.

The paper is organized as follows. In Section 2 we present the main components of our proposal: first, the rules for identifying XY/Y pairs, and then two alternative methods for improving the coherence of the translation of a subsequent mention Y, one based on post-editing and the other one based on caching, which builds upon initial experiments presented by Mascarell et al. (2014). In Section 3, we present our experimental setting. In Section 4, we evaluate our proposal on ZH/EN and DE/FR translation, demonstrating that the translation of nouns is indeed improved, mainly by automatic or human comparisons with the reference translation. We conclude with a brief discussion of related studies (Section 5) and with perspectives for future work (Section 6).

2 Description of the Method

2.1 Overview

We propose to use the translation of a compound XY to improve the translation of a subsequent occurrence of Y, the head of the XY noun phrase, in the following way, represented schematically in Figure 1 (details for each stage are given below).

First, the presence of XY/Y patterns is detected either by examining whether a compound XY is followed by an occurrence of Y, or, conversely, by examining for each Y candidate whether it appears as part of a previous compound XY. Distance constraints and additional filtering rules are implemented to increase the likelihood that XY and Y are actually co-referent, or at least refer to entities of the same type.

Second, each sentence is translated by a baseline SMT system, and the translation of the head Y of each compound XY is identified using the word alignment from the SMT decoder. This translation is used as the translation of a subsequent occurrence of Y either by caching the corresponding source/target word pair in the SMT or by post-editing the baseline SMT output. For instance, if the Chinese pair (蔬菜, 菜) is identified, where the first compound can unambiguously be translated into English by 'vegetable', then the translation of a subsequent occurrence of 菜 is enforced to 'vegetable'. This has the potential to improve over the baseline translation, because when considered individually, 菜 could also be translated as 'dish', 'greens', 'wild herbs', etc.

2.2 Identifying XY/Y Pairs

Chinese and German share a number of similarities regarding compounds. Although Chinese texts are not word-segmented, once this operation is performed, multi-character words in which all characters have individual meanings – such as the above-mentioned 蔬菜 ('vegetable') – are frequent. Similarly, in German, noun-noun compounds such as 'Bundesamt' ('Bund' + 'Amt', for Federal Bureau) or Nordwand ('Nord' + 'Wand', for North face) are frequent as well. While the identification of XY noun-noun compounds is straightforward with morpho-syntactic analysis tools, the identification of a subsequent mention of the head noun, Y, and especially the decision whether this Y refers or not to the same entity XY, are more challenging issues. In other words, the main difficulty is to separate true XY/Y pairs from false positives.

To detect truly coreferent XY/Y pairs we narrow down the set of detected cases using handwritten rules that check the local context of Y. For example, only the cases where Y is preceded by demonstrative pronouns (e.g. 这 or 那 meaning 'this' and 'that' in Chinese, or 'diese' in German), possessive pronouns and determiners ('der', 'die', 'das' in German) are considered. Since other words can occur between the two parts (like classifiers in Chinese or adjectives), there are additional distance constraints: the pronoun or determiner must be separated by fewer than three words. Since the rules use morphological information and word boundaries, they are preceded by word segmentation[1] and tagging[2] for Chinese and morphological analysis for German.[3] For example, in the input sentence from Figure 1, we determine that the noun phrase 鞋 fits our condition for extraction as Y because as there are words before it which fulfill the condition for acceptance.

2.3 Enforcing the Translation of Y

Two language-independent methods have been designed to ensure that the translations of XY and Y are a consistent: post-editing and caching. The second one builds upon an earlier proposal tested only on DE/FR with subjective evaluations (Mascarell et al., 2014).

In the post-editing method, for each XY/Y pair, the translations of XY and Y by a baseline SMT system (see Section 3) are first identified through word alignment. We verify if the translations of Y in both noun phrases are identical or different. Both elements comprising the compound structure XY/Y are identified, for the standard cases, with only one possible XY referring to one Y. The translation of both words are provided by the baseline SMT system, and our system subsequently verifies if the translations of Y in both noun phrases are identical or different. We keep them intact in the first case, while in the second case we replace the translation of Y by the translation of XY or by its head noun only, if it contains several words. In the example in Figure 1, XY is translated into 'high heel' and Y into 'shoes', which is a wrong translation of 鞋 in this context. Using the consistency constraint, our method post-edits the translation of Y replacing it with 'heel', which is the correct word.

Several differences from the ideal case presented above must be handled separately. First, it may occur that several XY are likely co-referent with the same Y. In this case, if their translations differ, given that we cannot resolve the coreference, we do not post-edit Y.[4] If the translations of the several occurrences of XY are the same, but consist of one word, we still do not post-edit Y. We only change it if the translations consist of several words, ensuring that XY is a compound noun phrase. Second, if the compound XY is not translated (out-of-vocabulary word), we do not post-edit Y.[5] Third, sometimes the alignment of Y is empty in the target sentence (alignment error or untranslated word), in which case we apply post-editing as above on the word preceding Y, if it is aligned.

In the caching method (Mascarell et al., 2014), once an XY compound is identified, we obtain the translation of the Y part of the compound through the word alignment given by the SMT decoder. Next, we check that this translation appears as a translation of Y in the phrase table, and if so, we cache both Y and the obtained translation. We then enforce the cached translation every time a coreference Y to XY is identified. Note that this is different from the probabilistic caching proposed by Tiedemann (2010), because in our case the cached translation is deterministically enforced as the translation of Y.

3 Experimental Settings

The experiments are carried out on two different parallel corpora: the WIT[3] Chinese-English dataset (Cettolo et al., 2012) with transcripts of TED lectures and their translations, and the Text+Berg German-French corpus (Bubenhofer et al., 2013), a collection of articles from the year-

[1] Using the Stanford Word Segmenter available from http://nlp.stanford.edu/software/segmenter.shtml.

[2] Using the Stanford Log-linear Part-of-speech Tagger, http://nlp.stanford.edu/software/tagger.shtml.

[3] Using Gertwol (Koskeniemmi and Haapalainen, 1994).

[4] Upon manual examination, we found that using the most recent XY was not a reliable candidate for the antecedent.

[5] In fact, we can use the translation of Y as a translation candidate for XY. Our observations show that this helps to improve BLEU scores, but does not affect the specific scoring of Y in Section 4.

		Sentences	Tokens
ZH	Training	188'758	19'880'790
	Tuning	2'457	260'770
	Testing	855	12'344
DE	Training	285'877	5'194'622
	Tuning	1'557	32'649
	Testing	505	12'499

Table 1: Sizes of SMT data sets.

books of the Swiss Alpine Club. The sizes of the subsets used for training, tuning and testing the SMT systems are given in Table 1. The test sets were constructed by selecting all the sentences or fragments which contained the XY/Y pairs, identified as above, to maximize their number in the test data, given that they are not needed in the training/tuning sets, as the proposed methods are not based on machine learning.

The rules for selecting coreferent XY/Y pairs in Chinese identified 261 pairs among 192k sentences. The rather low rate of occurrence (about one every 700 sentences) is explained by the strict conditions of the selection rules, which are designed to maximize the likelihood of coreference. In German, less restrictive rules selected 7,365 XY/Y pairs (a rate of one every 40 sentences). Still, in what follows, we randomly selected 261 XY/Y pairs for the DE/FR test data, to match their number in the ZH/EN test data.

Our baseline SMT system is the Moses phrase-based decoder (Koehn et al., 2007), trained over tokenized and true-cased data. The language models were built using SRILM (Stolcke et al., 2011) at order 3 (i.e. up to trigrams) using the default smoothing method (i.e. Good-Turing). Optimization was done using Minimum Error Rate Training (Och, 2003) as provided with Moses.

The effectiveness of proposed systems is measured in two ways. First, we use BLEU (Papineni et al., 2002) for overall evaluation, to verify whether our systems provide better translation for entire texts. Then, we focus on the XY/Y pairs and count the number of cases in which the translations of Y match the reference or not, which can be computed automatically using the alignments.

However, the automatic comparison of a system's translation with the reference is not entirely informative, because even if the two differ, the system's translation can still be acceptable. Therefore, we analyzed these "undecided" situations manually, with three human annotators (among the authors of the paper). The annotators rated separately the system's translations of Y and the reference ones as 'good', 'acceptable' or 'wrong'.

4 Analysis of Results

4.1 Automatic Comparison with a Reference

The BLEU scores obtained by the baseline SMT, the caching and post-editing methods, and an oracle system are given in Table 2. The scores are in the same range as the baseline scores found by other teams on these datasets (Cettolo et al., 2012, Table 7 for ZH/EN), and much higher on DE/FR than ZH/EN.

Our methods have a small positive effect on ZH/EN translation, and a small negative effect on DE/FR one. Given the sparsity of XY/Y pairs with respect to the total number of words, hence the small number of changed words, these results meet our prior expectations. Indeed, we also computed the oracle BLEU scores for both language pairs, i.e. the scores when all Y members of XY/Y pairs are (manually) translated exactly as in the reference (last line of Table 2). These values are only slightly higher than the other scores, showing that even a perfect translation of the Y nouns would only have a small effect on BLEU.

	ZH/EN	DE/FR
BASELINE	11.18	27.65
CACHING	11.23	27.26
POST-EDITING	11.27	27.48
ORACLE	11.30	27.80

Table 2: BLEU scores of our methods.

We now turn to the reference-based evaluation of the translations of Y in the 261 XY/Y pairs, comparing the baseline SMT with each of our methods. These results are represented as four contingency tables – two language pairs and two methods against the baseline – gathered together as percentages in Table 3. Among these values, we focus first on the total of pairs where one of our systems agrees with the reference while the baseline system does not (i.e., improvements due to the system), and the converse case (degradations). The higher the difference between the two values, the more beneficial our method.

For ZH/EN and the post-editing system, among the 222 extracted pairs, there were 45 improvements (20.3%) of the system with respect to the

			Caching		Post-editing	
			= ref	≠ ref	= ref	≠ ref
ZH/EN	Baseline	= ref	59.3	*4.1*	42.3	*4.5*
		≠ ref	**13.8**	22.8	**20.3**	32.9
DE/FR	Baseline	= ref	70.1	*10.3*	73.9	*5.0*
		≠ ref	**4.3**	15.2	**3.5**	17.5

Table 3: Comparison of each approach with the baseline, for the two language pairs, in terms of Y nouns which are identical or different from a reference translation ('ref'). All scores are percentages of the totals. Numbers in **bold** are improvements over the baseline, while those in *italics* are degradations.

baseline, and only 10 degradations (4.5%). There were also 94 pairs (42.3%) for which the baseline and the post-edited system were equal to the reference. The remaining 73 pairs (32.9%) will be analyzed manually in the next section. Therefore, from a pure reference-based view, the post-edited system has a net improvement of 15.8% (absolute) over the baseline in dealing with the XY/Y pairs.

A similar pattern is observed with the other method, namely caching, again on ZH/EN translation: 13.8% improvements vs. 4.1% degradations. The difference (i.e. the net improvement) is slightly smaller in this case with respect to the post-editing method.

For DE/FR translation, both methods appear to score fewer improvements than degradations. There are more than 70% of the pairs which are translated correctly by the baseline and by both systems, which indicates that the potential for improvement is much smaller for DE/FR than for ZH/EN.

While the pattern of improvement between ZH/EN and DE/FR is similar for post-editing and for caching, for both language pairs the post-editing method has a larger difference between improvements and degradations than the caching method. This can be explained by a lower coverage of the latter method, since it only enforces a translation when it appears as one of the translation candidates for Y in the phrase table (Mascarell et al., 2014).

4.2 Manual Evaluation of Undecided Cases

When both the baseline and one of our systems generate translations of Y which differ from the reference, it is not possible to compare the translations without having them examined by human subjects. This was done for the 73 such cases of the ZH/EN post-editing system. Three of the authors, working independently, considered each translation from each system (in separate batches) with respect to the reference one, and rated its meaning on a 3-point scale: 2 (good), 1 (acceptable) or 0 (wrong). To estimate the inter-rater agreement, we computed the average absolute deviation[6] and found a value of 0.15, thus denoting very good agreement. Below, we group '2' and '1' answers into one category, called "acceptable", and compare them to '0' answers, i.e. wrong translations.

When both the baseline and the post-edited translations of Y differ from the reference, they can either be identical (49 cases) or different (24). In the former case, of course, neither of the systems outperforms the other. The interesting observation is that the relatively high number of such cases (49) is due to situations where the reference translation of noun Y is by a pronoun (40), which the systems have currently no possibility to generate from a noun in the source sentence. Manual evaluation shows that the systems' translations are correct in 36 out of 40 cases. This large number shows that the "quality" of the systems is actually higher than what can be inferred from Table 3 only. Conversely, in the 9 cases when the reference translation of Y is not a pronoun, only about half of the translations are correct.

In the latter case, when baseline and post-edited translations differ from the reference *and* among themselves (24 cases), it is legitimate to ask which of the two systems is better. Overall, 10 baseline translations are correct and 14 are wrong, whereas 23 post-edited translations are correct (or at least acceptable) and only one is wrong. The post-edited system thus clearly outperforms the baseline in this case. Similarly to the observation above, we note that among the 24 cases considered here, almost all (20) involve a reference translation of Y by a pronoun. In these cases, the baseline

[6] Average of $\frac{1}{3}\sum_{i=1}^{3} |\text{score}_i - \text{mean}|$ over all ratings .

system translates only about half of them with a correct noun (9 out of 20), while the post-edited system translates correctly 19 out of 20.

5 Related Work

We briefly review in this section several previous studies from which the present one has benefited. Our idea is built upon the one-sense-per-discourse hypothesis (Gale et al., 1992) and its application to machine translation is based on the premise that consistency in discourse (Carpuat, 2009) is desirable. The initial compound idea was first published by Mascarell et al. (2014), in which the coreference of compound noun phrases in German (e.g. Nordwand/Wand) was studied and used to improve DE/FR translation by assuming that the last constituent of the compound Y should share the same translation as that of Y in XY.

Several other approaches focused on enforcing consistent lexical choice. Tiedemann (2010) proposed a cache-model to enforce consistent translation of phrases across the document. However, caching is sensitive to error propagation, that is, when a phrase is incorrectly translated and cached, the model propagates the error to the following sentences. Gong et al. (2011) later extended Tiedemann's proposal by initializing the cache with phrase pairs from similar documents at the beginning of the translation and by also applying a topic cache, which was introduced to deal with the error propagation issue. Xiao et al. (2011) defined a three step procedure that enforces the consistent translation of ambiguous words, achieving improvements for EN/ZH. Ture et al. (2012) encouraged consistency for AR/EN MT by introducing cross-sentence consistency features to the translation model, while Alexandrescu and Kirchhoff (2009) enforced similar translations to sentences having a similar graph representation.

Our work is an instance of a recent trend aiming to go beyond sentence-by-sentence MT, by using semantic information from previous sentences to constrain or correct the decoding of the current one. In this paper, we compared caching and post-editing as ways of achieving this goal, but a document-level decoder such as Docent (Hardmeier et al., 2012) could be used as well. In other studies, factored translation models (Koehn and Hoang, 2007) have been used with the same purpose, by incorporating contextual information into labels used to indicate the meaning of ambiguous discourse connectives (Meyer and Popescu-Belis, 2012) or the expected tenses of verb phrase translations (Loaiciga et al., 2014). Quite naturally, there are analogies between our work and studies of pronoun translation (Le Nagard and Koehn, 2010; Hardmeier and Federico, 2010; Guillou, 2012), with the notable difference that pronominal anaphora resolution remains a challenging task. Finally, our work and its perspectives contribute to the general objective of using discourse-level information to improve MT (Hardmeier, 2014; Meyer, 2014).

6 Conclusion and Perspectives

We presented a method to enforce the consistent translation of coreferences to a compound, when the coreference matches the head noun of the compound. Experimental results showed that baseline SMT systems often translate coreferences to compounds consistently for DE/FR, but much less so for ZH/EN. For a significant number of cases in which the noun phrase Y had multiple meanings, our system reduced the frequency of mistranslations in comparison to the baseline, and improved noun phrase translation.

In this work, we considered XY/Y pairs, hypothesizing that when they are coreferent, they should have consistent translations. In the future, we will generalize this constraint to complex noun phrases which are not compounds. More generally, we will explore the encoding of coreference constraints into probabilistic models that can be combined with SMT systems, so that coreference constraints are considered in the decoding process.

Acknowledgments

The authors are grateful for the support of the Swiss National Science Foundation (SNSF) through the Sinergia project MODERN: Modeling Discourse Entities and Relations for Coherent Machine Translation, grant nr. CRSII2_147653 (`www.idiap.ch/project/modern`).

References

Andrei Alexandrescu and Katrin Kirchhoff. 2009. Graph-based learning for statistical machine translation. In *Proceedings of the Annual Conference of the North American Chapter of the Association for Computational Linguistics (NAACL)*, pages 119–127, Boulder, Colorado.

Noah Bubenhofer, Martin Volk, David Klaper, Manuela Weibel, and Daniel Wüest. 2013. Text+Berg-korpus (release 147_v03). Digitale Edition des Jahrbuch des SAC 1864-1923, Echo des Alpes 1872-1924 und Die Alpen 1925-2011.

Marine Carpuat. 2009. One Translation per Discourse. In *Proceedings of the Workshop on Semantic Evaluations: Recent Achievements and Future Directions (SEW)*, pages 19–27, Singapore.

Mauro Cettolo, Christian Girardi, and Marcello Federico. 2012. WIT^3: Web inventory of transcribed and translated talks. In *Proceedings of the 16th Conference of the European Association for Machine Translation (EAMT)*, pages 261–268, Trento, Italy.

William A Gale, Kenneth W Church, and David Yarowsky. 1992. One sense per discourse. In *Proceedings of the Workshop on Speech and Natural Language*, pages 233–237.

Zhengxian Gong, Min Zhang, and Guodong Zhou. 2011. Cache-based document-level statistical machine translation. In *Proceedings of the 2011 Conference on Empirical Methods in Natural Language Processing (EMNLP)*, pages 909–919, Edinburgh.

Liane Guillou. 2012. Improving pronoun translation for statistical machine translation. In *Proceedings of EACL 2012 Student Research Workshop (13th Conference of the European Chapter of the ACL)*, pages 1–10, Avignon, France.

Christian Hardmeier and Marcello Federico. 2010. Modelling Pronominal Anaphora in Statistical Machine Translation. In *Proceedings of International Workshop on Spoken Language Translation (IWSLT)*, Paris, France.

Christian Hardmeier, Joakim Nivre, and Jörg Tiedemann. 2012. Document-Wide Decoding for Phrase-Based Statistical Machine Translation. In *Proceedings of the Conference on Empirical Methods in Natural Language Processing and Natural Language Learning (EMNLP-CoNLL)*, Jeju, Korea.

Christian Hardmeier. 2014. *Discourse in Statistical Machine Translation*. PhD thesis, Uppsala University, Sweden.

Philipp Koehn and Hieu Hoang. 2007. Factored translation models. In *Proceedings of the Joint Conference on Empirical Methods in Natural Language Processing (EMNLP) and Computational Natural Language Learning (CONLL)*, pages 868–876, Prague, Czech Republic.

Philipp Koehn, Hieu Hoang, Alexandra Birch, Chris Callison-Burch, Marcello Federico, Nicola Bertoldi, Brooke Cowan, Wade Shen, Christine Moran, Richard Zens, Chris Dyer, Ondrej Bojar, Alexandra Constantin, and Evan Herbs. 2007. Moses: Open Source Toolkit for Statistical Machine Translation. In *Proceedings of 45th Annual Meeting of the Association for Computational Linguistics (ACL), Demonstration Session*, pages 177–180, Prague, Czech Republic.

Kimmo Koskeniemmi and Mariikka Haapalainen. 1994. Gertwol–lingsoft oy. *Linguistische Verifikation: Dokumentation zur Ersten Morpholympics*, pages 121–140.

Ronan Le Nagard and Philipp Koehn. 2010. Aiding pronoun translation with co-reference resolution. In *Proceedings of the Joint 5th Workshop on Statistical Machine Translation and Metrics (MATR)*, pages 258–267, Uppsala, Sweden.

Sharid Loaiciga, Thomas Meyer, and Andrei Popescu-Belis. 2014. English-French Verb Phrase Alignment in Europarl for Tense Translation Modeling. In *Proceedings of the 9th international conference on Language Resources and Evaluation (LREC)*, Reykjavik, Iceland.

Laura Mascarell, Mark Fishel, Natalia Korchagina, and Martin Volk. 2014. Enforcing consistent translation of German compound coreferences. In *Proceedings of the 12th Konvens Conference*, Hildesheim, Germany.

Thomas Meyer and Andrei Popescu-Belis. 2012. Using sense-labeled discourse connectives for statistical machine translation. In *Proceedings of the EACL 2012 Joint Workshop on Exploiting Synergies between IR and MT, and Hybrid Approaches to MT (ESIRMT-HyTra)*, pages 129–138, Avignon, France.

Thomas Meyer. 2014. *Discourse-level Features for Statistical Machine Translation*. PhD thesis, EPFL, Lausanne.

Franz Josef Och. 2003. Minimum Error Rate Training in Statistical Machine Translation. In *Proceedings of the 41st Annual Meeting of the Association for Computational Linguistics (ACL)*, pages 160–167, Sapporo, Japan.

Kishore Papineni, Salim Roukos, Todd Ard, and Wei-Jing Zhu. 2002. BLEU: a method for automatic evaluation of machine translation. In *Proceedings of the 40th Annual Meeting of the Association for Computational Linguistics (ACL)*.

Andreas Stolcke, Jing Zheng, Wen Wang, and Victor Abrash. 2011. SRILM at Sixteen: Update and Outlook. In *Proceedings of the IEEE Automatic Speech Recognition and Understanding Workshop (ASRU)*, Waikoloa, Hawaii.

Jörg Tiedemann. 2010. Context adaptation in statistical machine translation using models with exponentially decaying cache. In *Proceedings of the 2010 Workshop on Domain Adaptation for Natural Language Processing*, pages 8–15, Uppsala, Sweden.

Ferhan Ture, Douglas W. Oard, and Philip Resnik. 2012. Encouraging consistent translation choices. In *Proceedings of the 2012 Conference of the North*

American Chapter of the Association for Computational Linguistics: Human Language Technologies (NAACL-HLT), pages 417–426, Montréal, Canada.

Tong Xiao, Jingbo Zhu, Shujie Yao, and Hao Zhang. 2011. Document-level consistency verification in machine translation. In *Proceedings of the 13th Machine Translation Summit*, pages 131–138, Xiamen, China.

Learning representations for text-level discourse parsing

Gregor Weiss
Faculty of Computer and Information Science
University of Ljubljana
Večna pot 113, Ljubljana, Slovenia
gregor.weiss@student.uni-lj.si

Abstract

In the proposed doctoral work we will design an end-to-end approach for the challenging NLP task of text-level discourse parsing. Instead of depending on mostly hand-engineered sparse features and independent components for each subtask, we propose a unified approach completely based on deep learning architectures. To train more expressive representations that capture communicative functions and semantic roles of discourse units and relations between them, we will jointly learn all discourse parsing subtasks at different layers of our architecture and share their intermediate representations. By combining unsupervised training of word embeddings with our layer-wise multi-task learning of higher representations we hope to reach or even surpass performance of current state-of-the-art methods on annotated English corpora.

1 Introduction

Modern algorithms for natural language processing (NLP) are based on statistical machine learning and require a computationally convenient representation of input data. Unfortunately real-world plain text is usually represented as an unstructured sequence of words with complex relations between them. Therefore it is extremely important to discover good representations in the form of informative text features.

In NLP such features are almost always hand-engineered sparse features and require expensive human labor and expert knowledge to construct. They are usually based on lexicons or features extracted by other NLP subtasks and have the form of hand-engineered extraction rules, regular expressions, lemmatization, part-of-speech (POS) tags, positions or lengths of arguments, tense forms, syntactic parse trees, and similar. Although such features are specific for a given language, domain, and task, they work well enough for simple NLP tasks, like named entity recognition or POS tagging. Nevertheless, the ability to learn text features and representations automatically would have a lot of potential to improve state-of-the-art performance on more challenging NLP tasks, such as text-level discourse parsing. This may even be more important for languages where progress in NLP is still lacking.

Variants of deep learning architectures have been shown to provide a different approach to learning in which latent features are automatically learned as distributed dense vectors. They managed to represent meaningful relations with word (Collobert, 2011), POS and dependency tag (Chen and Manning, 2014), sentence (Guo and Diab, 2012), and document (Socher et al., 2012) embeddings and achieved surprising results for a number of NLP tasks. It has been shown that both unsupervised pre-training (Hinton et al., 2006) and multi-task learning (Collobert and Weston, 2008) significantly improve their performance in the absence of hand-engineered features. This makes them especially interesting for the problem of text-level discourse parsing.

2 Text-level discourse parsing

In natural language, a piece of text meant to communicate specific information, function, or knowledge (clauses, sentences, or even paragraphs) is called a discourse. They are often understood only in relation to other discourse units (at any level of grouping) and their combination creates a joint meaning larger than individual unit's meaning alone (Mann and Thompson, 1988).

Discourse parsing is the task of determining how these units are related to each other (like in Figure 1) and plays a central role in a num-

Proceedings of the ACL-IJCNLP 2015 Student Research Workshop, pages 16–21,
Beijing, China, July 28, 2015. ©2015 Association for Computational Linguistics

ber of high-impact natural language processing (NLP) applications, including text summarization, sentence compression, sentiment analysis, and question-answering. For analyzing different perspectives of discourse analysis researchers proposed a number of theoretical frameworks and released annotated corpora, such as RST Discourse Treebank (RST-DT) (Carlson et al., 2003) and Penn Discourse Treebank (PDTB) (Prasad et al., 2008). Both of these decompose discourse parsing into a few subtasks and, like in most of NLP, their success depends on expert knowledge of each subtask and hand-engineering of more powerful features (Feng and Hirst, 2012; Lin et al., 2014), representations, and heuristics (Joty et al., 2013; Prasad et al., 2010).

Despite recent progress in automatic discourse segmentation and sentence-level parsing (Fisher and Roark, 2007; Joty et al., 2012; Soricut and Marcu, 2003), text-level discourse parsing remains a significant challenge (Feng and Hirst, 2012; Ji and Eisenstein, 2014; Lin et al., 2014). Traditional hand-engineering approaches unfortunately seem to be insufficient, as discourses and relations between them do not follow any strict grammar or obvious rules.

Two main theoretical frameworks with English corpus have been proposed to capture different rhetorical characteristics, and serve different applications.

The Penn Discourse Treebank (PDTB) (Prasad et al., 2008) is currently the largest discourse-annotated corpus, consisting of 2159 articles from Wall Street Journal. It strives to maintain a theory-neutral approach by adopting the predicate-argument view and independence of discourse relations. In it either explicitly or implicitly given discourse connectives, such as coordinating conjunction (e.g. "and", "but"), subordinating conjunction (e.g. "if", "because"), or discourse adverbial (e.g. "however", "also"), combine pairs of discourse arguments into relations. For PDTB-style discourse parsing, extracting argument spans seems to be the most difficult subtask (Lin et al., 2014), resulting in the best overall performance of only 34.80% in F_1-measure (Kong et al., 2014).

The RST Discourse Treebank (RST-DT) (Carlson et al., 2003) follows the theoretical framework of Rhetorical Structure Theory (RST) (Mann and Thompson, 1988). It contains 385 annotated documents from the Wall Street Journal with 18 high-level categories and 110 fine-grained relations. Any coherent text can be represented as a RST discourse tree structure (like in Figure 1) whose leaves are minimal non-overlapping text spans called elementary discourse units. Adjacent nodes are joined depending on their discourse relations to form a tree. In a mono-nuclear discourse relation one of the text spans is the nucleus, which is more salient than the satellite, while in a multi-nuclear relation all text spans are equally important for interpretation. Performance of RST-style discourse parsing is evaluated based on their ability to locate spans of text that serve as arguments (best 85.7% in F_1-measure (Feng and Hirst, 2012)), identify which of the arguments is the nucleus (best 71.1% in F_1-measure (Ji and Eisenstein, 2014)), and tag the sense and location of discourse relations (best 61.6% in F_1-measure (Ji and Eisenstein, 2014)).

3 Related work

Early work on linguistic and computational discourse analysis produced several theoretical frameworks and one of the most influential is Rhetorical Structure Theory (RST) (Mann and Thompson, 1988). In order to automatically build a hierarchical structure of a text, first approaches (Marcu, 2000) relied mainly on discourse markers, hand-engineered rules, and heuristics. Learning-based approaches were first applied to identify within-sentence discourse relations (Soricut and Marcu, 2003), and only later to cross-sentence text-level relations (Baldridge and Lascarides, 2005). They largely focused on lexical, syntactic, and structural features, but the close relationship between discourse structure and semantic meaning suggests that this may not be sufficient (Prasad et al., 2008; Subba and Di Eugenio, 2009). Further work on discourse parsing focused first on having a binary classifier for determining whether two adjacent discourse units should be merged, followed by a multi-class classifier for determining which discourse relation should be assigned to the new subtree (DuVerle and Prendinger, 2009). Improved results (Feng and Hirst, 2012) have been achieved by incorporating rich linguistic features (Hernault et al., 2010), including lexical semantics, and specific discourse production rules (Lin et al., 2009). An alternative approach is based on jointly performing detection and classification in a bottom-

- [The dollar finished lower yesterday,] e_1 [after another session on Wall Street.] e_2
- [Concern about the volatile U.S. stock market had faded in recent sessions,] e_3 [and traders let the dollar languish in a narrow range until tomorrow,] e_4 [when the preliminary report on U.S. gross national product is released.] e_5
- [But movements in the Dow Jones Industrial Average yesterday put Wall Street back in the spotlight] e_6 [and inspired participants to bid the U.S. unit lower.] e_7

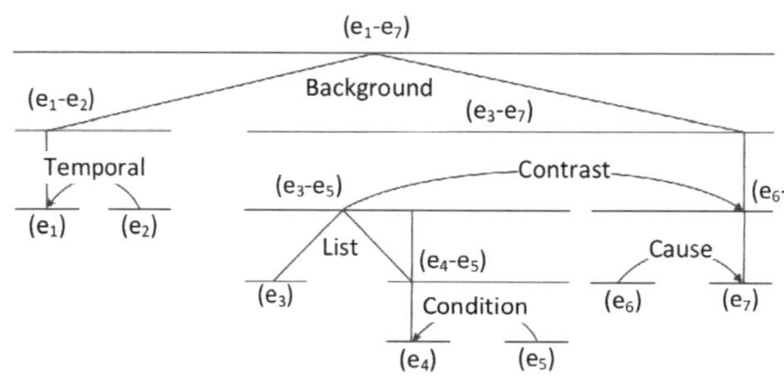

Figure 1: An example of seven elementary discourse units (e_1-e_7), and (mono- or multi-nuclear) relations between them in an RST discourse tree representation (Feng et al., 2014).

up fashion while distinguishing within-sentence and cross-sentence relations (Joty et al., 2013) and improved with discriminative reranking of discourse trees using tree kernels (Joty and Moschitti, 2014). It has been shown that constituent- and dependency-based syntax and features based on coreference links improve performance (Surdeanu et al., 2015). The first PDTB-style end-to-end discourse parser (Lin et al., 2014) uses a connective list to identify explicit candidates, followed by simple features and parse trees to extract arguments and identify discourse relations. Classifying implicit discourse relations can be improved by combining distributed representations of parse trees with coreferent entity mentions (Ji and Eisenstein, 2015). Extracting discourse arguments has been attempted by using classic linear word tagging with conditional random fields and global features (Ghosh et al., 2012), identifying nodes in constituent subtrees (Lin et al., 2014), and hybrid merging and pruning of parse trees with integer linear programming (Kong et al., 2014).

Deep learning architectures consist of multiple layers of simple learning blocks stacked on each other and, when well trained, tend to do a better job at disentangling the underlying factors of variation. Beginning with raw data, its representation is transformed into increasingly higher and more abstract forms in each layer, until the final low-dimensional features or representation useful for a given task is reached. Their success is possible with breakthroughs and improvements in training techniques (like AdaGrad or Adam optimization, rectifier function, dropout regularization) and with initialization using unsupervised pre-training (Hinton et al., 2006; Collobert, 2011) on massive datasets (such as Wikipedia or Wall Street Journal). Pre-training helps deep networks to develop natural abstractions and combined with multi-task learning (Collobert and Weston, 2008) it can significantly improve their performance in the absence of hand-engineered features.

Classic feed-forward architectures are inappropriate for processing text documents, because of their variable length and natural representation as a sequence of words. One approach to solve this is to specify a transition-based processing mechanism (Chen and Manning, 2014; Ji and Eisenstein, 2014) and train a neural network classifier to make parsing decisions. Recurrent neural networks (RNNs) (Elman, 1990) or their generalization, recursive neural networks (Goller and Küchler, 1996), represent a more direct approach by recursively applying the same set of weights over the sequence (temporal dimension) or structure (tree-based). Li et al. (Li et al., 2015) have recently showed that only some NLP tasks benefit from recursive models applied on syntactic parse trees and recurrent models seem to be sufficient for discourse parsing. By stacking multiple hidden layers into a deep RNN makes them represent a temporal hierarchy with multiple layers operating at different time scales (Hermans and Schrauwen, 2013). Learning to store information over extended time intervals has been achieved with long short-term memory (Hochreiter and Schmidhuber, 1997), time delay neural network (Waibel et al., 1989), or neural Turing machines (Graves et al., 2014). Bidirectional variants of these models can incorporate information from preceding as well as following tokens (Schuster and Paliwal, 1997). Recursive neural networks have also been shown to support different task-specific representations, such as matrix-vector representation of words (Socher et al., 2012) or recurrent neural tensor networks (Socher et al., 2013). For our discourse parsing task such deeper models, that can learn abstract representations on different time scales, might better model the discourse relations between input vectors and (hopefully) capture their communicative functions and semantic meaning.

A few initial attempts of applying representation learning to our task have already shown substantial performance improvements over previous state-of-the-art. Ji and Eisenstein (Ji and Eisenstein, 2014) implement a shift-reduce discourse parser on top of given RST-style discourse units to simultaneously learn parsing and a discourse-driven projection of features using support vector machines with gradient-based updates. Li et al. (Li, 2014) produce a distributed representation of RST-style discourse units using recursive convolution on sentence parse trees and apply a classifier to determine relations between them. Ji and Eisenstein (Ji and Eisenstein, 2014) also improved classification of PDTB-style implicit discourse relations by combining distributed representations of parse trees with coreferent entity mentions.

4 Contribution to science

Because text-level discourse parsing is an important, yet still challenging NLP task, it is the focus of our doctoral dissertation.

Method for text-level discourse parsing. Instead of depending on mostly hand-engineered sparse features and independent separately-developed components for each subtask, we propose a unified end-to-end approach for text-level discourse parsing completely based on deep learning architectures. First each of the discourse parsing subtasks, such as argument boundary detection, labeling, discourse relation identification and sense classification, need to be formulated in terms of RNNs and similar derivable learning architectures. To benefit from their ability to learn intermediate representations they will be partially stacked on top of each order, such that the last but one layer (i.e. output layer) for each subtask is shared with other subtasks. By placing increasingly more difficult subtasks at different layers in one deep architecture, they can benefit from each others intermediate representations, improve robustness and training speed. Figure 2 further combines unsupervised training of word embeddings with our layer-wise multi-task learning of higher representations and illustrates our goal of a unified end-to-end approach for text-level discourse parsing utilizing different layers of representations.

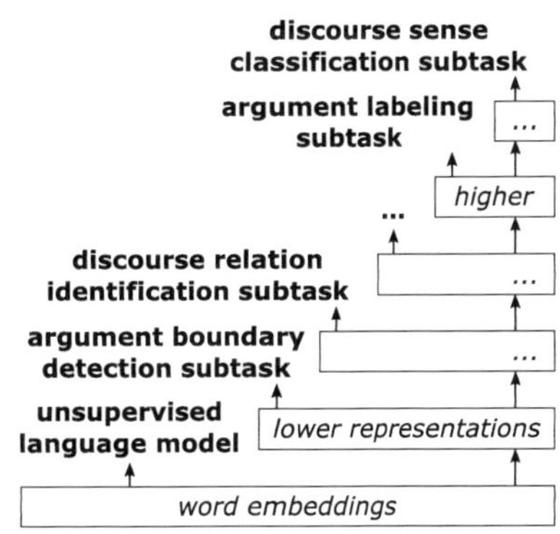

Figure 2: Illustration of our unified end-to-end approach for text-level discourse parsing with layer-wise multi-task learning of higher representations.

5 Work plan

To accomplish this we will, on one hand, need to find the best deep learning models for each of the discourse parsing subtasks, suitable architecture, activation functions, and figure out how to adapt them to operate on sequential data and with each other. This includes analyzing deep learning architectures, identifying their strengths, useful components, and their suitability for our NLP task.

Afterwards combine them into one unified deep learning architecture with shared intermediate representations and unsupervised training of word embeddings. Developing a prototype for shallow discourse parsing will open the door for find the best initialization procedures, training functions, learning rates, and similar. Shallow PDTB-style discourse parsing is also a challenge on this years CoNLL 2015 conference, where adjacent text spans are not necessarily connected with discourse relations to form a tree.

Additionally we will experiment with new and more expressive representations and structures (like neural tensor networks) that could capture communicative functions and semantic roles of discourse units and relations between them.

Even though our method could be applied to any plain text, we plan on evaluating it on standard annotated English corpora. After applying our approach on at lest one of the corpora, we intend to qualitatively analyze the identified discourse units and relations between them to gain insights about its strengths and weaknesses. On the other hand, the dataset will allow us to also quantitatively compare its performance to current state-of-the-art methods. The procedure for our method will begin by pre-training the weights in our deep architecture on external unlabeled datasets (like Wikipedia), than jointly train on all discourse parsing subtasks on the training set, use a separate validation set to optimize hyper-parameters, and estimate its performance on the test set. For evaluation purposes standard evaluation measures for subtasks based on F_1-scores will be used.

6 Conclusion

To increase the generality of our unified end-to-end approach for text-level discourse parsing, we will try to depend as little as possible on background knowledge in the form of hand-engineered features for a specific language, domain, or task. By incorporating various improvements in automatic learning of features and representations we hope to reach or even surpass performance of current state-of-the-art methods on annotated English corpora.

References

Jason Baldridge and Alex Lascarides. 2005. Probabilistic head-driven parsing for discourse structure. In *Proc. 9th Conf. Comput. Nat. Lang. Learn.*, pages 96–103. Association for Computational Linguistics.

Lynn Carlson, Daniel Marcu, and Mary Ellen Okurowski. 2003. Building a discourse-tagged corpus in the framework of Rhetorical Structure Theory. *Curr. New Dir. Discourse Dialogue*, 22:85–112.

Danqi Chen and Christopher D Manning. 2014. A Fast and Accurate Dependency Parser using Neural Networks. In *Proc. 2014 Conf. Empir. Methods Nat. Lang. Process.*, pages 740–750.

Ronan Collobert and Jason Weston. 2008. A Unified Architecture for Natural Language Processing: Deep Neural Networks with Multitask Learning. In *Proc. 25th Int. Conf. Mach. Learn.*, volume 20, pages 160–167.

Ronan Collobert. 2011. Deep Learning for Efficient Discriminative Parsing. *Int. Conf. Artif. Intell. Stat.*, 15:224–232.

David A. DuVerle and Helmut Prendinger. 2009. A novel discourse parser based on support vector machine classification. In *Proc. Jt. Conf. 47th Annu. Meet. ACL 4th Int. Jt. Conf. Nat. Lang. Process. AFNLP*, pages 665–673. Association for Computational Linguistics.

Jeffrey L. Elman. 1990. Finding structure in time* 1. *Cogn. Sci.*, 14(1990):179–211.

Vanessa Wei Feng and Graeme Hirst. 2012. Text-level Discourse Parsing with Rich Linguistic Features. In *Proc. 50th Annu. Meet. Assoc. Comput. Linguist.*, pages 60–68. Association for Computational Linguistics.

Vanessa Wei Feng, Ziheng Lin, and Graeme Hirst. 2014. The Impact of Deep Hierarchical Discourse Structures in the Evaluation of Text Coherence. In *Proc. 25th Int. Conf. Comput. Linguist.*

Seeger Fisher and Brian Roark. 2007. The utility of parse-derived features for automatic discourse segmentation. In *Proc. 45th Annu. Meet. Assoc. Comput. Linguist.*, volume 45, pages 488–495.

Sucheta Ghosh, Giuseppe Riccardi, and Richard Johansson. 2012. Global features for shallow discourse parsing. In *Annu. Meet. Spec. Interes. Gr. Discourse Dialogue*, pages 150–159.

Christoph Goller and Andreas Küchler. 1996. Learning Task-Dependent Distributed Representations by Backpropagation Through Structure. In *IEEE Int. Conf. Neural Networks*, pages 347–352.

Alex Graves, Greg Wayne, and Ivo Denihelka. 2014. Neural Turing Machines. *arXiv Prepr. arXiv410.5401*, pages 1–26.

Weiwei Guo and Mona Diab. 2012. Modeling Sentences in the Latent Space. In *Proc. 50th Annu. Meet. Assoc. Comput. Linguist.*, pages 864–872. Association for Computational Linguistics.

Michiel Hermans and Benjamin Schrauwen. 2013. Training and Analyzing Deep Recurrent Neural Networks. In *Adv. Neural Inf. Process. Syst.*, volume 26, pages 190–198.

Hugo Hernault, Helmut Prendinger, David A. DuVerle, and Mitsuru Ishizuka. 2010. HILDA: A Discourse Parser Using Support Vector Machine Classification. *Dialogue and Discourse*, 1(3):1–33.

Geoffrey E. Hinton, Simon Osindero, and Yee-Whye Teh. 2006. A Fast Learning Algorithm for Deep Belief Nets. *Neural Comput.*, 18:1527–1554.

Sepp Hochreiter and Jürgen Schmidhuber. 1997. Long Short-Term Memory. *Neural Comput.*, 9(8):1735–1780.

Yangfeng Ji and Jacob Eisenstein. 2014. Representation Learning for Text-level Discourse Parsing. In *Proc. 52nd Annu. Meet. Assoc. Comput. Linguist.*, pages 13–24.

Yangfeng Ji and Jacob Eisenstein. 2015. One Vector is Not Enough: Entity-Augmented Distributed Semantics for Discourse Relations. *Trans. Assoc. Comput. Linguist.*

Shafiq Joty and Alessandro Moschitti. 2014. Discriminative Reranking of Discourse Parses Using Tree Kernels. In *Proc. 2014 Conf. Empir. Methods Nat. Lang. Process.*, pages 2049–2060.

Shafiq Joty, Giuseppe Carenini, and Raymond T. Ng. 2012. A novel discriminative framework for sentence-level discourse analysis. In *Proc. 2012 Jt. Conf. Empir. Methods Nat. Lang. Process. Comput. Nat. Lang. Learn.*, pages 904–915. Association for Computational Linguistics.

Shafiq Joty, Giuseppe Carenini, Raymond T. Ng, and Yashar Mehdad. 2013. Combining Intra- and Multi-sentential Rhetorical Parsing for Document-level Discourse Analysis. In *Proc. 51st Annu. Meet. Assoc. Comput. Linguist.*, pages 486–496.

Fang Kong, Hwee Tou, and Ng Guodong. 2014. A Constituent-Based Approach to Argument Labeling with Joint Inference in Discourse Parsing. In *Conf. Empir. Methods Nat. Lang. Process.*, pages 68–77.

Jiwei Li, Dan Jurafsky, and Eduard Hovy. 2015. When Are Tree Structures Necessary for Deep Learning of Representations? *Arxiv*.

Junyi Jessy Li. 2014. Reducing Sparsity Improves the Recognition of Implicit Discourse Relations. In *Proc. SIGDIAL 2014 Conf.*, number June, pages 199–207.

Ziheng Lin, Min-yen Kan, and Hwee Tou Ng. 2009. Recognizing Implicit Discourse Relations in the Penn Discourse Treebank. In *Proc. 2009 Conf. Empir. Methods Nat. Lang. Process.*, pages 343–351. Association for Computational Linguistics.

Ziheng Lin, Hwee Tou Ng, and Min-Yen Kan. 2014. A PDTB-Styled End-to-End Discourse Parser. *Nat. Lang. Eng.*, 20(2):151–184.

William C. Mann and Sandra A. Thompson. 1988. Rhetorical structure theory: Toward a functional theory of text organization. *Text-Interdisciplinary J. Study Discourse*, 8(3):243–281.

Daniel Marcu. 2000. The Rhetorical Parsing of Unrestricted Texts: A Surface-based Approach. *Comput. Linguist.*, 26(38):395–448.

Rashmi Prasad, Nikhil Dinesh, Alan Lee, Eleni Miltsakaki, Livio Robaldo, Aravind Joshi, and Bonnie Webber. 2008. The Penn Discourse TreeBank 2.0. *Proc. Sixth Int. Conf. Lang. Resour. Eval.*, pages 2961–2968.

Rashmi Prasad, Aravind Joshi, and Bonnie Webber. 2010. Exploiting Scope for Shallow Discourse Parsing. In *Int. Conf. Lang. Resour. Eval.*, pages 2076–2083.

Mike Schuster and Kuldip K Paliwal. 1997. Bidirectional recurrent neural networks. *IEEE Trans. Signal Process.*, 45(11):2673–2681.

Richard Socher, Brody Huval, Christopher D. Manning, and Andrew Y. Ng. 2012. Semantic Compositionality through Recursive Matrix-Vector Spaces. In *Proc. 2012 Jt. Conf. Empir. Methods Nat. Lang. Process. Comput. Nat. Lang. Learn.*, pages 1201–1211. Association for Computational Linguistics.

Richard Socher, Alex Perelygin, Jean Y. Wu, Jason Chuang, Christopher D. Manning, Andrew Y. Ng, and Christopher Potts. 2013. Recursive deep models for semantic compositionality over a sentiment treebank. In *Proc. Conf. Empir. Methods Nat. Lang. Process.*, pages 1631–1642.

Radu Soricut and Daniel Marcu. 2003. Sentence level discourse parsing using syntactic and lexical information. *Proc. 2003 Conf. North Am. Chapter Assoc. Comput. Linguist. Hum. Lang. Technol.*, 1:228–235.

Rajen Subba and Barbara Di Eugenio. 2009. An effective discourse parser that uses rich linguistic information. In *Proc. Hum. Lang. Technol. 2009 Annu. Conf. North Am. Chapter Assoc. Comput. Linguist.*, pages 566–574. Association for Computational Linguistics.

Mihai Surdeanu, Thomas Hicks, and Marco A. Valenzuela-Escarcega. 2015. Two Practical Rhetorical Structure Theory Parsers. In *Proc. North Am. Chapter Assoc. Comput. Linguist.*

Alexander Waibel, Toshiyuki Hanazawa, Geoffrey E. Hinton, Kiyohiro Shikano, and Kevin J. Lang. 1989. Phoneme recognition using time-delay neural networks. *IEEE Trans. Acoust.*, 37(3):328–339.

Transition-based Dependency DAG Parsing Using Dynamic Oracles

Alper Tokgöz
Istanbul Technical University
Department of Computer Engineering
Istanbul, Turkey
tokgoza@itu.edu.tr

Gülşen Eryiğit
Istanbul Technical University
Department of Computer Engineering
Istanbul, Turkey
gulsen.cebiroglu@itu.edu.tr

Abstract

In most of the dependency parsing studies, dependency relations within a sentence are often presented as a tree structure. Whilst the tree structure is sufficient to represent the surface relations, deep dependencies which may result to multi-headed relations require more general dependency structures, namely Directed Acyclic Graphs (DAGs). This study proposes a new dependency DAG parsing approach which uses a dynamic oracle within a shift-reduce transition-based parsing framework. Although there is still room for improvement on performance with more feature engineering, we already obtain competitive performances compared to static oracles as a result of our initial experiments conducted on the ITU-METU-Sabancı Turkish Treebank (IMST).

1 Introduction

Syntactic parsing is the process of determining the grammatical structure of a sentence as conforming to the grammatical rules of the relevant natural language. The structure of the sentence is determined according to the grammar formalism that the parser is built upon. Phrase structure parsers, also known as constituency parsers, parse a sentence by splitting it into its smaller constituents. On the other hand, in dependency parsers, the structure of the sentence is represented as dependency trees consisting of directed dependency links between a dependent and a head word.

Data-driven dependency parsing frameworks have gained increasing popularity in recent years and been used in a wide range of applications such as machine translation (Ding and Palmer, 2005), textual entailment (Yuret et al., 2013) and question answering (Xu et al., 2014). Most data-driven dependency parsers achieve state-of-the art parsing performances with a language agnostic approach on the different syntactic structures of different languages (Buchholz and Marsi, 2006). Modern data-driven dependency parsers can be categorized into two groups: graph-based and transition-based parsers. Graph-based parsers rely on the global optimization of models aiming to find spanning trees over dependency graphs. On the other hand, transition-based parsers work basically with greedy local decisions that are deterministically selected by oracles, which are generic machine learning models trained to make decisions about the next transition action. In a recent study, Zhang and Nivre (2012) propose a new approach on transition-based parsing that aims to provide global learning instead of greedy local decisions.

Despite the high performances of both graph-based and transition-based dependency parsers, these are generally bounded by the constraint that each dependent may not have multiple heads. Therefore, the resulting parsing output is a tree where words correspond to nodes and dependency relations correspond to edges. Although dependency trees yield satisfactory performances, they are inadequate in capturing dependencies at different levels of semantic interpretations or more complicated linguistic phenomena (e.g. relative clauses, anaphoric references) which could result in multi-head dependencies together with existing surface dependency relations. An example is given in Figure 1 which is taken from the Turkish IMST Treebank (Sulubacak and Eryiğit, 2015). In Figure 1, the dependent token "Umut" depends

Proceedings of the ACL-IJCNLP 2015 Student Research Workshop, pages 22–27,
Beijing, China, July 28, 2015. ©2015 Association for Computational Linguistics

on more than one head token with SUBJECT relations: 1) the verb "*koşmak*" (to run) and 2) the verb "*düşmek*" (to fall). Adding a second relation (emphasized with a dash-dotted line in the figure) to the token "Umut" breaks the condition that each token may have at most one head, and renders existing dependency tree parsers incompatible for this setup. It is also worth mentioning that the deep dependencies in the IMST are not discriminated from surface dependencies by the use of different labels.

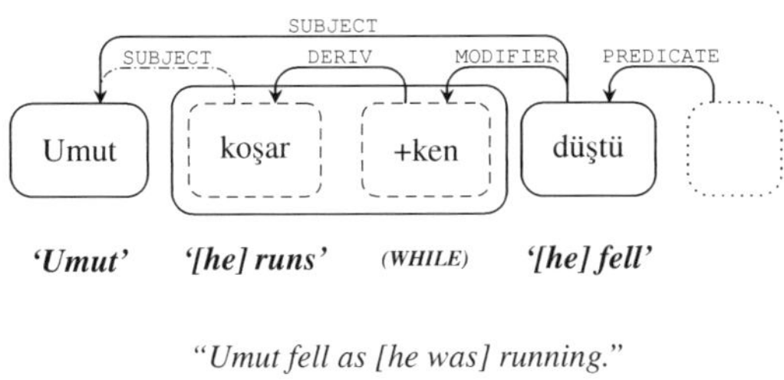

Figure 1: Example for Turkish multi-head dependencies.

In this paper, for the first time in the literature, we investigate the impact of using dynamic oracles for parsing multi-head dependency structures by extending the approach of Goldberg and Nivre (2012). We provide comparisons with the replication of the basic shift-reduce DAG parsing algorithm of Sagae and Tsujii (2008) and a first time implementation of their proposed arc-eager parsing algorithm. The remainder of the paper first gives a background information about the topic, then introduces the DAG parsing framework and the proposed algorithms together with experiments and results.

2 Background

Although it is possible to discover the syntactic relations with a two stage model by first finding the regular surface dependencies and then finding the deep relations with post-processing as in Nivre et al. (2010), it is not always straightforward to decide which dependencies should be treated as surface relations or deep relations as in the case of Turkish. Thus, in this study, we focus on single stage models and aim to discover the entire set of relations in a single pass. McDonald and Pereira (2006) use graph-based algorithms for DAG parsing simply using approximate interference in an edge-factored dependency model starting from dependency trees. On the other hand, Sagae and Tsujii (2008) propose a transition-based counterpart for DAG parsing which made available for parsing multi-headed relations. They modified the existing shift-reduce bottom-up dependency parsing algorithm of Nivre and Nilsson (2005) to allow multiple heads per token by the use of cycle removal and pseudo-projectivization as a preprocessing stage. They report higher performance scores on the Danish treebank compared to McDonald and Pereira (2006).

A standard way of determining transition actions in a shift-reduce dependency parser is using static oracles. During the training stage, the learning instances for the oracle are prepared by the use of manually annotated gold-standard parse trees and the current parsing configuration. During the parsing stage, the already trained oracle decides on the next transition operation. One of the problems with static oracles lays beneath the spurious ambiguity, which implies there might be more than one transition sequence for a given sentence and the sequence proposed by an oracle may not be the easiest to learn. The second problem occurs when the parser makes a parsing error which leads to a parser configuration from which the correct parse tree is not derivable. The algorithm does not provide any solutions for dealing with the error propagation caused by such situations. The idea of dynamic oracles introduced by Goldberg and Nivre (2012) rises for handling the aforementioned handicaps of static oracles. Rather than returning a unique transition for a given configuration, a dynamic oracle returns a set of valid transitions regarding the current configuration, which would allow the algorithm to explore non-optimal configurations during the training procedure.

3 Transition-Based Solutions for Dependency DAG Parsing

Transition-based parsing frameworks consider the transition system to be an abstract machine that processes input sentences and produces corresponding parsing graphs. The tokens of the input sequence and the partially created dependency structures are kept within the following data structures:

1. a buffer β which includes the remaining unprocessed tokens in the input sequence in a queue,

2. a stack σ which consists of the tokens being processed,

3. a set A of assigned dependency arcs.

The transition actions explained in the following subsections are basic stack and queue operations that correspond to parsing actions marking dependency relations. The algorithm starts with a buffer β initialized with all tokens of a sentence preserving their sequence, and an empty stack σ. The parsing process finishes when there are no nodes left in β and only the artificial root in σ.

3.1 Basic shift-reduce parsing with multiple heads

The first algorithm that is capable of parsing DAG structures is the standard algorithm of Sagae and Tsujii (2008). The complete list of the transitions of this algorithm is as follows:

- Shift: Pops the first item of the buffer and pushes it onto the top of the stack.
- Left-Reduce: Pops the top two items of the stack, creates a left arc between them where the top item is assigned as the head of the item below, and pushes the head token back onto the stack.
- Right-Reduce: Pops the top two items of the stack, creates a right arc between them, where the item below is assigned as the head of the top item, and pushes the head token back onto the stack.
- Left-Attach: Creates a left arc between the top two items of the stack, where the top item is assigned as the head of the one below. The stack and the buffer remain unchanged.
- Right-Attach: Creates a right dependency arc between the two top items on the stack and assigns the top token as the dependent of the token below. As the second step, it pops the top of the stack and places it into the buffer β.

3.2 Multi-Head Arc-Eager Parsing Algorithm

The second transition algorithm introduced but not implemented by Sagae and Tsujii (2008) is a variation of the Arc-Eager algorithm of Nivre et al. (2007) and has the following transition operations:

- Shift: Pops the first item of the buffer and pushes it onto the top token of the stack.
- Left-Arc: Creates a left dependency arc between the top token of the stack and the first token of the input buffer, where the first token in the buffer becomes the head and the one at the top of the stack becomes the dependent. It is also worth noticing that the stack and the input buffer remains unchanged.
- Right-Arc: Creates a right dependency arc between the top token of the stack and the first token on the input buffer, where the token in the stack becomes the head, and the token which is in front of the buffer becomes the dependent. It is also worth noticing that the stack and the input buffer remains unchanged.
- Reduce: Pops the top item of the stack if and only if it was previously associated with at least one head.

3.3 Multi-Head Arc Eager Parsing with a Dynamic Oracle

In order to design a dynamic oracle with the capability of parsing multi-head dependencies, we need an efficient method for computing the cost of each transition. To this end, we extend the dynamic oracle defined by Goldberg and Nivre (2012), considering DAG parsing arc-eager system of Sagae and Tsujii (2008). Extended arc-eager transition system will operate in the same way as previously defined in Section 3.2, within a dynamic oracle system whose cost function is defined with a transition operation, the current configuration $c = (\sigma|s, b|\beta, A)$[1] and the gold parse of the sentence (G_{gold}). Differing from Goldberg and Nivre (2012), for ease of computation, we prefer marking transitions as zero cost or costly instead of computing the exact cost:

- $Cost(LeftAttach, c, G_{gold})$ Attaching s to b with a left arc is costly, if there is a right arc between s and b, or it is already attached with a left arc.
- $Cost(RightAttach, c, G_{gold})$ Attaching s to b by creating right arc is costly, if there is a left arc between s and b, or it is already attached with a right arc.

[1] In $c = (\sigma|s, b|\beta, A)$, s denotes the top token of the stack σ, b denotes first item of buffer β, A denotes revealed arcs

- $Cost(Reduce, c, G_{gold})$ Popping s from the stack means it will be no longer possible to associate it with any head or dependent from buffer β, therefore it is costly if it has heads or dependents in the β.

- $Cost(Shift, c, G_{gold})$ Pushing b onto the stack means it will be no longer possible to associate it with any heads or dependents in stack σ, therefore it is costly if it has a head or dependent token in the σ.

Since left attach and right attach operations do not change the parser configuration (i.e. these operations cannot lead to a parser configuration from which the gold tree is not reachable), their cost is measured according to the validity of the attachment. The only difference of our multi-head variant from the single head arc-eager transition system is that the left and right arc operations do not change the parser state. As such, it is essentially a relaxed version of the single-head system. Therefore, since the arc-decomposition property holds for the single-head system (as proven by Goldberg and Nivre (2013)), it also holds for our variant.

We use the same online training procedure (with the perceptron algorithm) as Goldberg and Nivre (2012) given in Algorithm 1.

Algorithm 1 Online training with dynamic oracle

1: **procedure** TRAIN
2:     $w \leftarrow 0$
3:     **for** $I \leftarrow 1$, ITERATIONS **do**
4:         $c \leftarrow c_s(x)$
5:         **for** sentence x **do**
6:             **while** c is not terminal **do**
7:                 $t_p \leftarrow argmax_t w.\Phi(c, t)$
8:                 $ZC \leftarrow \{t | o(t; c; G_{gold}) = \textbf{true}\}$
9:                 $t_o \leftarrow argmax_{t \epsilon ZC} w.\Phi(c, t)$
10:                 **if** $t_p \notin ZC$ **then**
11:                     $w \leftarrow w + \Phi(c, t_o) - \Phi(c, t_p)$
12:                 $t_n \leftarrow$NEXT(I, t_p, ZC)
13:                 $c \leftarrow t_n(c)$
14: **procedure** NEXT(I, t, ZC)
15:     **if** $t \in ZC$ **then**
16:         **return** t
17:     **else**
18:         $RANDOM\_ELEMENT(ZC)$

The proposed oracle will return a set of zero cost transition operations (denoted as ZC at line 8) where the costs are calculated according to the cost function defined above. Feature weights will be updated only if the perceptron model makes a transition prediction that does not belong to the zero cost transitions (lines 10 and 11). After that, the next transition operation is chosen by the function NEXT, which returns the transition that is predicted by the model if it belongs to zero cost transitions; if not, it returns a random transition which belongs to the zero cost transition set.

4 Experiments

In order to apply the specified DAG parsing algorithm to non-projective sentences, a pseudo-projective transformation operation is applied to the IMST. For that aim, we apply Head scheme[2] described by Nivre (2005). Moreover, before the application of this pseudo-projective transformation, the cyclic dependency paths are handled as described by Sagae and Tsujii (2008), by reversing the shortest arc within the cyclic dependency path until no cyclic path remains. 99.3% precision and 99.2% recall are acquired on IMST by applying the pseudo-projective transformation and detransformation operations. As a learning component, we follow the work of Sagae and Tsujii (2008) and use a Maximum Entropy model for the classification with the greedy search algorithm. For the dynamic oracle experiment, we use an averaged perceptron algorithm iterating 15 times over the training data.

The following features are used in all of the experiments:

- The POS tag, lemma and morphological features of the top 3 tokens on the stack and the first 3 tokens in the buffer.

- The POS tag and dependency relations of the rightmost and leftmost modifiers of the top 2 items on the stack.

- The number of heads and dependents of the top item of the stack and the first item of the buffer.

- The dependency relations of the top of the stack.

[2] Although other schemes could be tried for DAGs for better performance, this is left for future work due to time constraints.

- Whether the top 2 tokens on the stack have a dependency relation between them or not.
- Whether the top token of the stack and the first of the buffer have a dependency relation between them or not, and if so the direction and the type of the relation.
- Combination of the surface form of the top token of the stack and its number of left and right modifiers.
- Combination of the surface form of the first token of the buffer and its number of left and right modifiers.
- The surface forms and POS tags of heads of the top token of the stack and the first token of the buffer.
- The previous two parsing actions.

For training and evaluation purposes, we use the IMST with ten-fold cross validation. Experiment results are given in Table 4.

Table 1: Unlabeled scores of experiments with using IMST.

Experiment	Precision	Recall	F1
Static-Standard	79.42	77.56	78.50
Static-Eager	78.90	76.79	77.83
Dynamic-Eager	79.68	81.17	80.42

As shown in Table 4, the static arc-eager DAG implementation for Turkish performs slightly worse than the arc-standard algorithm. This is not surprising in the light of previous studies (Nivre, 2008; Eryiğit et al., 2008) reporting that the arc standard algorithm performs better in tree parsing due to the smaller number of classes to be learned by the oracle. However, the proposed multi-head arc-eager algorithm with dynamic oracle (referred to as Dynamic-Eager) yields the best precision, recall and F1 scores among the three experiments.[3]

In this study, although there is still room for improvement on performance with more feature engineering, we obtain better results on Turkish IMST treebank between static and dynamic oracles with our newly proposed method for parsing DAGs. This encourages us to test our system with different languages as future work with the expectation that the ameliorations will be much higher than the reported ones in the single-head scenario.

[3]The difference of this model from the runner-up models are found to be statistically significant according to McNemar's test ($p < 0.0001$)

5 Conclusion and Future Works

In this paper, we experimented with three different transition-based algorithms for DAG parsing which eliminate the single-head constraint of traditional algorithms and allows multi-head dependency relations to represent more complicated linguistic phenomena along with surface relations. We present the first results for arc-eager DAG parsing with static oracles and propose a new arc-eager DAG parsing algorithm using dynamic oracles. Our initial experiments conducted on Turkish pave the way for future research on the usage of the dynamic arc-eager DAG parsing for other languages. For future work, we will first conduct experiments on how well the Dynamic-Eager algorithm performs on different treebanks, including multi-head dependencies (such as the Danish treebank (Kromann, 2003)). Secondly, we will conduct experiments on previously described static-oracle parsing algorithms by using different classifiers such as Support Vector Machines.

Acknowledgments

We hereby acknowledge that this study is part of a research project named "Parsing Web 2.0 Sentences" that is supported by TÜBİTAK (Turkish Scientific and Technological Research Council) 1001 program (grant number 112E276) and part of the ICT COST Action IC 1207.

References

Sabine Buchholz and Erwin Marsi. 2006. Conll-x shared task on multilingual dependency parsing. In *Proceedings of the Tenth Conference on Computational Natural Language Learning*, pages 149–164. Association for Computational Linguistics.

Yuan Ding and Martha Palmer. 2005. Machine translation using probabilistic synchronous dependency insertion grammars. In *Proceedings of the 43rd Annual Meeting on Association for Computational Linguistics*, pages 541–548. Association for Computational Linguistics.

Gülşen Eryiğit, Joakim Nivre, and Kemal Oflazer. 2008. Dependency parsing of Turkish. *Computational Linguistics*, 34(3):357–389.

Yoav Goldberg and Joakim Nivre. 2012. A dynamic oracle for arc-eager dependency parsing. In *COLING*, pages 959–976.

Yoav Goldberg and Joakim Nivre. 2013. Training deterministic parsers with non-deterministic oracles. *Transactions of the association for Computational Linguistics*, 1:403–414.

Matthias T Kromann. 2003. The danish dependency treebank and the underlying linguistic theory. In *Proc. of the Second Workshop on Treebanks and Linguistic Theories (TLT)*.

Ryan T McDonald and Fernando CN Pereira. 2006. Online learning of approximate dependency parsing algorithms. In *EACL*. Citeseer.

Joakim Nivre and Jens Nilsson. 2005. Pseudo-projective dependency parsing. In *Proceedings of the 43rd Annual Meeting on Association for Computational Linguistics*, pages 99–106. Association for Computational Linguistics.

Joakim Nivre, Johan Hall, Jens Nilsson, Atanas Chanev, Gülsen Eryigit, Sandra Kübler, Svetoslav Marinov, and Erwin Marsi. 2007. Maltparser: A language-independent system for data-driven dependency parsing. *Natural Language Engineering*, 13(02):95–135.

Joakim Nivre, Laura Rimell, Ryan McDonald, and Carlos Gomez-Rodriguez. 2010. Evaluation of dependency parsers on unbounded dependencies. In *Proceedings of the 23rd International Conference on Computational Linguistics*, pages 833–841. Association for Computational Linguistics.

Joakim Nivre. 2008. Algorithms for deterministic incremental dependency parsing. *Computational Linguistics*, 34(4):513–553.

Kenji Sagae and Jun'ichi Tsujii. 2008. Shift-reduce dependency DAG parsing. In *Proceedings of the 22nd International Conference on Computational Linguistics-Volume 1*, pages 753–760. Association for Computational Linguistics.

Umut Sulubacak and Gülşen Eryiğit. 2015. A redefined Turkish dependency grammar and its implementations: A new Turkish web treebank & the revised Turkish treebank. under review.

Kun Xu, Sheng Zhang, Yansong Feng, and Dongyan Zhao. 2014. Answering natural language questions via phrasal semantic parsing. In *Natural Language Processing and Chinese Computing*, pages 333–344. Springer.

Deniz Yuret, Laura Rimell, and Aydın Han. 2013. Parser evaluation using textual entailments. *Language resources and evaluation*, 47(3):639–659.

Yue Zhang and Joakim Nivre. 2012. Analyzing the effect of global learning and beam-search on transition-based dependency parsing. In *COLING (Posters)*, pages 1391–1400.

Disease Event Detection based on Deep Modality Analysis

Yoshiaki Kitagawa †, Mamoru Komachi †, Eiji Aramaki ‡,
Naoaki Okazaki §, and Hiroshi Ishikawa †

† Tokyo Metropolitan University {kitagawa-yoshiaki at ed., komachi at, ishikawa-hiroshi at}tmu.ac.jp
‡ Kyoto University eiji.aramaki at gmail.com
§ Tohoku University okazaki at ecei.tohoku.ac.jp

Abstract

Social media has attracted attention because of its potential for extraction of information of various types. For example, information collected from Twitter enables us to build useful applications such as predicting an epidemic of influenza. However, using text information from social media poses challenges for event detection because of the unreliable nature of user-generated texts, which often include counter-factual statements.

Consequently, this study proposes the use of modality features to improve disease event detection from Twitter messages, or "tweets". Experimental results demonstrate that the combination of a modality dictionary and a modality analyzer improves the F1-score by 3.5 points.

1 Introduction

The rapidly increasing popularity of Social Networking Services (SNSs) such as Twitter and Facebook has greatly eased the dissemination of information. Such data can serve as a valuable information resource for various applications. For instance, Huberman et al. (2009) investigated actual linked structures of human networks, Boyd et al. (2010) mapped out retweeting as a conversational practice, and Sakaki et al. (2010) detected earthquakes using SNSs.

An important and widespread application of SNS mining is in the public health field such as infection detection. Among various infectious diseases, influenza is one of the most important diseases worldwide.

However, it is difficult to estimate the precise number of influenza-infected patients based on naïve textual features because SNS messages that contain the word "flu" might not necessarily refer to being infected with influenza. The following tweets are examples of such cases:

(1) I **might** have the flu.

(2) **If** I had the flu, I **would** be forced to rest.

"might" in example (1) suggests that there is only a suspicion of having influenza. Similarly, "if" in example (2) shows that the person is not actually infected.

To filter these instances, we propose to integrate two modalities of information into factuality analysis: shallow modality analysis based on a surface string match and deep modality analysis based on predicate-argument structure analysis. The main contribution of this paper is two-fold:

- We annotate a new dataset extracted from Twitter for flu detection and prediction task, and extend the naïve bag-of-words model of Aramaki et al. (2011) and propose several Twitter-specific features for disease event detection tasks.
- We show that modality information contributes to the factuality analysis in influenza-related tweets, which demonstrates the basic feasibility of the proposed approach. All features presented in this paper increase recall.

2 Related work

The task of influenza detection and prediction originates from the work of Serfling (1963) in epidemiology who tried to define a threshold for influenza breakout.

Since then, various approaches have been proposed for influenza detection and prediction (Groendyke et al., 2011; Moreno et al., 2002; Mugglin et al., 2002).

During the last decade, web-mining approaches have been proposed to detect influenza bursts in

Proceedings of the ACL-IJCNLP 2015 Student Research Workshop, pages 28–34,
Beijing, China, July 28, 2015. ©2015 Association for Computational Linguistics

Table 1: Examples of annotated data.

label	tweet
positive	やっぱり**インフルエンザ**だったか…こりゃ家族内で蔓延しそうだな... English translation: After all I was infected with **flu** ... This virus is likely to spread in the family.
negative	まぁ俺**インフルエンザ**のワクチンとか打ったことないんですけどね English translation: Well, I'd never got a preventive shot against **flu**.

their early stages. Two sources of people's behavior have been mainly employed: (1) web search queries (such as Yahoo! search (Polgreen et al., 2008) and Google search (Ginsberg et al., 2009)), and (2) activity logs of SNSs. This study specifically examines the latter because of the availability and accessibility of data.

Twitter is the SNS that is most frequently used for influenza detection (Achrekar et al., 2012; Aramaki et al., 2011; Ji et al., 2012; Sadilek et al., 2012; Lamb, 2013). Previous research on the subject has revealed a high correlation ratio between the number of influenza patients and actual tweets related to influenza.

It is possible to obtain large amounts of data from Twitter texts, but the main challenge is to filter noise from this data. For example, Aramaki et al. (2011) reported that half of the tweets containing the word "cold (disease)" simply mention some information about a disease, but do not refer to the actual eventuality of having the disease.

To address that problem, a classifier was produced to ascertain the factuality of the disease event. This paper follows that approach, using modality analysis, which provides a strong clue for factuality analysis (Saurí and Pustejovsky, 2012).

Modality has been used and discussed in various places. Li et al. (2014) employ such modality features, although they do not describe the effect of using modality features in web application tasks. Furthermore, several workshops have been organized around the use of specific modalities, such as Negation and Speculation (e.g. NeSP-NLP[1]). In this study, we use generic modality features to improve factuality analysis.

[1] www.clips.ua.ac.be/NeSpNLP2010/

3 Modality analysis for disease event detection

3.1 Task and data

The disease event detection task is a binary classification task to extract/differentiate whether the writer or the person around the writer is infected with influenza or not. However, because of the inherently noisy nature of tweets, some tweet messages are unrelated to influenza infection even when the messages include the word "flu." Therefore, we adopt a supervised approach first proposed by Aramaki et al. (2011).

We annotate a tweet with a binary label (influenza positive and negative), as in prior studies (Aramaki et al., 2011) [2]. If a tweet writer (or anybody near the writer) is infected with influenza, then the label is positive. Otherwise, the label is negative. Additionally, we save the time stamp when the tweet was posted online. Table 1 presents some examples. For this study, we use 10,443 Japanese tweet messages including the word "flu." In this dataset, the number of positive examples is 1,319; the number of negative examples is 9,124.

Because language heavily relies on modality to judge the factuality of sentences, modality analysis is a necessary process for factuality analysis (Matsuyoshi et al., 2010b). In line with this observation, we propose two ways to incorporate modality analysis for factuality analysis.

3.2 Shallow modality feature

In Japanese, multiple words can serve as a function word as a whole (Matsuyoshi et al., 2007). We designate them as "functional expressions." Even though functional expressions often carry modality information, previous works including Aramaki et al. (2011) do not consider functional expressions that comprise several words. Therefore,

[2] These data are used for training an influenza web surveillance service "Mr.influ" http://mednlp.jp/influ/.

Table 2: Sense ID feature based on Tsutsuji.

tweet	sense ID
インフルエンザ **ですか**... びっくり **し** ま **し** た。 English translation: You **were** infected **with** flu... I was surprised.	**で**→ r32 **です**→ D41 **か**→ Q31 **し**→ n13 (The words such us "**were**" and "**with**" are converted to sense IDs.)

Table 3: Extended modality feature based on Zunda.

tweet	extended modality
隣の患者さんが**インフルエンザ** **発覚** English translation: I **found out** that the patient next to me had the flu.	**発覚**=成立 **found out** = happened

we use the hierarchically organized dictionary of Japanese functional expressions, "Tsutsuji[3]," as the first approach.

Tsutsuji provides surface forms of 16,801 entries. In addition, it classifies them hierarchically. Each node in the hierarchy has a sense ID. We use the sense ID of Tsutsuji as a shallow semantic feature to capture the modality of the main predicate in tweets. To find functional expressions related to influenza, we use this feature when a functional expression in Tsutsuji is found within 15 characters to the right context of "flu." Table 2 presents an example of a tweet and the sense ID feature assigned by Tsutsuji.

3.3 Deep modality feature

To incorporate deep modality analysis, we use the output of the Japanese Extended Modality Analyzer, "Zunda,[4]" which analyzes modality such as authenticity judgments (whether the event has happened) and virtual event (whether it is an assumption or a story) with respect to the context of the events (verbs, adjective, and event-nouns). It is trained on the Extended Modality Corpus (Matsuyoshi et al., 2010a) using rich linguistic features such as dependency and predicate–argument structural analysis. It complements the dictionary-based shallow modality feature described in the previous section.

Specifically, Zunda grasps the modality information such us negation and speculation. See the following example:

(1) インフルエンザに**かかって** **ない**。(English translation: I am **not** *infected* with influenza.)

(2) インフルエンザに**かかった** **かもしれない**。(English translation: I **might** be *infected* with influenza.)

For this example, Zunda detects that "infected" is an event and judges the probability of it describing an event. For example (1) and (2), Zunda respectively outputs "not happened" and "high probability happened".

We consider verbs and event-nouns that follow the word "flu" to be related to influenza infection. In addition, we assign the estimated modality to them as a deep modality feature. Table 3 presents an example of a tweet and the estimated modality feature assigned by Zunda.

Table 4: Result of binary classification for disease event detection.

feature	Prec.	Rec.	F1-score
BoW	74.0	30.5	43.2
BoW+URL	69.9	31.3	43.2
BoW+Atmark	74.0	30.5	43.2
BoW+N-gram	70.7	34.5	46.4
BoW+Season	72.4	33.3	45.6
BoW+Tsutsuji	76.4	32.1	45.2
BoW+Zunda	69.9	31.3	43.2
baseline	69.7	39.2	50.2
baseline+Tsutsuji	70.2	42.0	**52.6**
baseline+Zunda	67.9	41.2	**51.3**
All	68.9	44.0	**53.7**

4 Experiment of disease event detection

4.1 Evaluation and tools

Considering our purpose of disease event detection, it is important to estimate the number of positive instances for flu correctly. In contrast, it is

[3]Tsutsuji: Japanese functional expressions dictionary `http://kotoba.nuee.nagoya-u.ac.jp/tsutsuji/`

[4]Zunda: extended modality analyzer `https://code.google.com/p/zunda/`

Table 5: Contribution and error analysis of shallow modality features.

Example 1 (correct example)	@* 強力な**インフルエンザ** **らしく** てですね, まだまだ完治しておりませぬ English translation: @* The flu is apparently terrible and I have not recovered yet.
Example 2 (false positive)	@* おかえびもずくさん、**インフル**流行っ**て** る **から** 手洗いうがいしてね English translation: @* The flu is going around, so you should wash hands and gargle.
Example 3 (false negative)	まさかの**インフルエンザ**... 全身鳥肌 **と** 震 **え** 半端ない寒気が... English translation: I can not believe I have the flu! I have goose bumps. I shiver and feel so cold... .

Table 6: Examples of deep modality feature with large weight. English translations are given in parentheses.

feature	weight	feature	weight
罹患=成立 (infection = happened)	0.80	注射=成立 (injection = happened)	-0.62
かかり=成立 (infect = happened)	0.65	対策=成立 (countermeasure = happened)	-0.50
診断=成立 (diagnosis = happened)	0.52	かかり=0 (infection = 0)	-0.48
寝=成立 (sleep = happened)	0.47	なる=成立 (become = happened)	-0.45
発覚=成立 (revelation = happened)	0.47	する=成立 (do = happened)	-0.45
回復=成立 (recovery = happened)	0.44	死亡=成立 (death = happened)	-0.42
ダウン=成立 (down = happened)	0.40	行っ=成立 (perform = happened)	-0.39
うつっ=成立 (give = happened)	0.39	注意=成立 (attention = happened)	-0.38
潜伏=成立 (incubation = happened)	0.37	感染=不成立 (infection = not happened)	-0.37

less important to predict the number of negative instances, although our system has high accuracy (about 91%). Therefore, we computed the precision, recall, and F1-score as the evaluation metrics and conducted five-fold cross-validation.

We used Classias (ver.1.1) [5] with its default setting to train the model. We applied L2-regularized logistic regression as a training algorithm. We used MeCab (ver.0.996) with IPADic (ver.2.7.0) as a morphological analyzer.

4.2 Feature

The features used for the experiments are presented below. These features are not modality features. We selected these features by performing preliminary experiments. Here, we omit the description related to modality features because the details are described in Section 3.

BoW: Bag of Words features of six morphemes around the "flu."

N-gram (character N-gram): Feature of character N-gram around the word "flu." The value of N is 1–4.

URL: Binary feature of the presence or absence of URL in messages.

Atmark: Binary feature of the presence or absence of reply in messages.

[5] Classias: `http://www.chokkan.org/software/classias/`

Table 7: Contribution and error analysis of deep modality features.

Example 4 (correct example)	10 年ぶりに**インフルエンザ**というものに **かかり** ました wwww English translation: It's been 10 years since I last had the flu, but now I have one (LOL).
Example 5 (false positive)	ASPARAGUS 渡邊忍が**インフルエンザ**に **感染** してしまい、本日の柏 DOMe でのライブは中止します。 English translation: Watanabe of ASPARAGUS is infected with flu, and today's concert in Kashiwa Dome has been canceled.
Example 6 (false negative)	**インフル**とな…おだいじに＼(^○^)／ English translation: So you have a flu... . Take care.:)

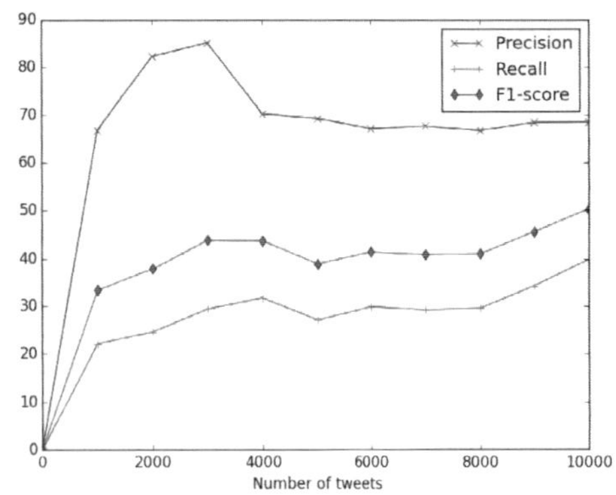

Figure 1: Learning curve for disease event detection.

Season: Binary feature of whether posting time is within December through February or not.

4.3 Baseline

For disease event detection, we follow previous studies Aramaki et al. (2011, 2012) to build the baseline classifier using a supervised approach. The baseline is constructed by combining all features except the modality features.

4.4 Experimental results

The result of disease event detection is shown in Table 4. Overall, they seem to have low recall and F1-Score. However, it turns out to be difficult to achieve high recall because the percentage of positive cases is extremely low (about 12.6%).

As shown, N-gram and Season features improve F1-score. Although the shallow modality feature boosts both precision and recall, the deep modality feature only improves recall in compensation with precision. The highest recall for the F1-score is achieved when using both shallow and deep modality features from Tsutsuji and Zunda (in the case of "All"). This result underscores the utility of the modality features for classifying a post by its factuality.

In addition, to judge the performance with respect to the amount of data, we plot a learning curve in Figure 1. Although the decision changes only slightly, recall tends to improve by increasing the amount of data.

5 Discussion

As described in this paper, we demonstrate the contribution of modality analysis for disease event detection. In what follows, we conduct error analysis of our proposed method.

5.1 Contribution and error analysis for shallow modality

Table 5 shows the correct and incorrect examples for the shallow modality. Example 1 is a correct example. In this case, we convert "らしく" ("seem") into sense ID; the classifier outputs an appropriate label. Example 2 is an example of false positive. Example 3 is an example of a false negative. Both examples are incorrect because they are assigned wrong sense IDs. That point illustrates the limitations of a simple string match, which does not take the context into account. It is necessary to perform word sense disambiguation for modality-related words.

5.2 Contribution and error analysis for deep modality

Next, we examine the deep modality features. Table 6 presents results of the deep modality features sorted by weight in descending order.

In many cases, the features can be understood intuitively compared to those of shallow modality features. Among the posts including the word "flu," posts about disease warnings, posts about vaccinations, and posts about epidemic news account for a large proportion. This tendency is exhibited clearly when one assigns negative weights. Positive weights include many event-nouns and verbs that are related directly to the disease.

Table 7 presents correct and incorrect examples for deep modality. Example 4 is a correct example. The deep modality feature "infection = happened" makes it possible to judge Example 4 correctly. Deep modality features appear to be critical in many cases, but in some cases they do not function as expected. Example 5 is an example of a false positive. Because of the "infection = happened" feature, the classifier judges it positive. However, not the writer, but a well-known figure (Watanabe of ASPARAGUS) has been infected with influenza. This is a common mistake that the classifier makes. This result indicates the importance of identifying the entity that is involved in a disease event. Furthermore, our classifier is not robust for non-event problems. Example 6 is an example of false positive. This example does not have the argument of an event. It is the characteristics of the colloquial sentence. Such examples can often be found in web documents.

6 Conclusion

This study examined a disease event detection method incorporating both shallow and deep modality features. Results show that the modality features improve the accuracy of the influenza detection. Although we have demonstrated that our method is useful for particular disease event detections, we must still ascertain whether it is applicable for other infectious diseases such as norovirus and dengue.

As future work, we would like to disambiguate functional expressions using sequence labeling techniques (Utsuro et al., 2007); we would also like to identify the predicate–argument structure of disease events (Kanouchi et al., 2015). Apart from that, an information extraction approach that looks for more specific patterns should be verified. Finally, we would like to adopt these findings to improve the prediction of epidemics.

Acknowledgments

We thank anonymous reviewers for their constructive comments, which have helped us to improve the manuscript.

References

Harshavardhan Achrekar, Avinash Gandhe, Ross Lazarus, Ssu-Hsin Yu, and Benyuan Liu. 2012. Twitter improves seasonal influenza prediction. In *International Conference on Health Informatics*, pages 61–70.

Eiji Aramaki, Sachiko Masukawa, and Mizuki Morita. 2011. Twitter catches the flu: detecting influenza epidemics using Twitter. In *Proceedings of the 16th Conference on Empirical Methods in Natural Language Processing*, pages 1568–1576.

Eiji Aramaki, Sachiko Masukawa, and Mizuki Morita. 2012. Microblog-based infectious disease detection using document classification and infectious disease model. *Journal of Natural Langage Proccessing*, 19(5):419–435.

Danah Boyd, Scott Golder, and Gilad Lotan. 2010. Tweet, tweet, retweet: Conversational aspects of retweeting on Twitter. In *Proceedings of the 2010 43rd Hawaii International Conference on System Sciences*, pages 1–10.

Jeremy Ginsberg, Matthew H Mohebbi, Rajan S Patel, Lynnette Brammer, Mark S Smolinski, and Larry Brilliant. 2009. Detecting influenza epidemics using search engine query data. *Nature*, 457(7232):1012–1014.

Chris Groendyke, David Welch, and David R Hunter. 2011. Bayesian inference for contact networks given epidemic data. *Scandinavian Journal of Statistics*, 38(3):600–616.

Bernardo A Huberman, Daniel M Romero, and Fang Wu. 2009. Social networks that matter: Twitter under the microscope. *First Monday*, 14(1):1–9.

Xiang Ji, Soon Ae Chun, and James Geller. 2012. Epidemic outbreak and spread detection system based on Twitter data. In *Health Information Science*, pages 152–163.

Shin Kanouchi, Mamoru Komachi, Naoaki Okazaki, Eiji Aramaki, and Hiroshi Ishikawa. 2015. Who caught a cold? - identifying the subject of a symptom. In *Proceedings of 53rd Annual Meeting of the Association for Computational Linguistics*.

Hubert Horace Lamb. 2013. *Climate: Present, Past and Future: Volume 1: Fundamentals and Climate Now*. Routledge.

Jiwei Li, Alan Ritter, Claire Cardie, and Eduard Hovy. 2014. Major life event extraction from Twitter based on congratulations/condolences speech acts. In *Proceedings of the 19th Conferences on Empirical Methods in Natural Language Processing*, pages 1997–2007.

Suguru Matsuyoshi, Satoshi Sato, and Takehito Utsuro. 2007. A Dictionary of Japanese Functional Expressions with Hierarchical Organization. *Journal of Natural Langage Proccessing*, 14(5):123–146.

Suguru Matsuyoshi, Megumi Eguchi, Chitose Sao, Koji Murakami, Kentaro Inui, and Yuji Matsumoto. 2010a. Annotating event mentions in text with modality, focus, and source information. In *Proceedings of the Seventh International Conference on Language Resources and Evaluation (LREC)*, pages 1456–1463.

Suguru Matsuyoshi, Megumi Eguchi, Chitose Sao, Koji Murakami, Kentaro Inui, and Yuji Matsumoto. 2010b. Factuality annotation for textual information analysis. *The IEICE Transactions on Information an Systems*, 93(6):705–713.

Yamir Moreno, Romualdo Pastor-Satorras, and Alessandro Vespignani. 2002. Epidemic outbreaks in complex heterogeneous networks. *The European Physical Journal B-Condensed Matter and Complex Systems*, 26(4):521–529.

Andrew S Mugglin, Noel Cressie, and Islay Gemmell. 2002. Hierarchical statistical modelling of influenza epidemic dynamics in space and time. *Statistics in medicine*, 21(18):2703–2721.

Philip M Polgreen, Yiling Chen, David M Pennock, Forrest D Nelson, and Robert A Weinstein. 2008. Using internet searches for influenza surveillance. *Clinical infectious diseases*, 47(11):1443–1448.

Adam Sadilek, Henry Kautz, and Jeffrey P Bigham. 2012. Finding your friends and following them to where you are. In *Proceedings of the fifth ACM international conference on web search and data mining*, pages 723–732.

Takeshi Sakaki, Makoto Okazaki, and Yutaka Matsuo. 2010. Earthquake shakes Twitter users: real-time event detection by social sensors. In *Proceedings of the 19th international conference on World wide web*, pages 851–860.

Roser Saurí and James Pustejovsky. 2012. Are you sure that this happened? Assessing the factuality degree of events in text. *Computational Linguistics*, 38(2):261–299.

Robert E Serfling. 1963. Methods for current statistical analysis of excess pneumonia-influenza deaths. *Public health reports*, 78(6):494.

Takehito Utsuro, Takao Shime, Masatoshi Tsuchiya, Suguru Matsuyoshi, and Satoshi Sato. 2007. Chunking and dependency analysis of japanese compound functional expressions by machine learning. In *Proceedings of 10th International Conference on Text, Speech and Dialogue (TSD)*.

Evaluation Dataset and System for Japanese Lexical Simplification

Tomoyuki Kajiwara
Department of Electrical Engineering
Nagaoka University of Technology
Nagaoka City, Niigata, Japan
kajiwara@jnlp.org

Kazuhide Yamamoto
Department of Electrical Engineering
Nagaoka University of Technology
Nagaoka City, Niigata, Japan
yamamoto@jnlp.org

Abstract

We have constructed two research resources of Japanese lexical simplification. One is a simplification system that supports reading comprehension of a wide range of readers, including children and language learners. The other is a dataset for evaluation that enables open discussions with other systems. Both the system and the dataset are made available providing the first such resources for the Japanese language.

1 Introduction

Lexical simplification is a technique that substitutes a complex word or phrase in a sentence with a simpler synonym. This technique supports the reading comprehension of a wide range of readers, including children (Belder and Moens, 2010; Kajiwara et al., 2013) and language learners (Eom et al., 2012; Moku et al., 2012).

The recent years have seen a great activity in this field of inquiry, especially for English: At the SemEval-2012 workshop, many systems were participating in the English lexical simplification task (Specia et al., 2012), for which also an evaluation dataset was constructed. Other resources for statistical learning of simplified rules were built, drawing on the Simple English Wikipedia (Zhu et al., 2010; Horn et al., 2014), e.g. several parallel corpora aligning standard and simple English (Zhu et al., 2010; Kauchak, 2013)[1,2] and evaluation datasets (Specia et al., 2012; Belder and Moens, 2012)[3,4].

On the other hand, there have been no published resources on Japanese lexical simplification so far. Such resources had to be created and made public, for the sake of readers in need of reading assistance, as well as to accelerate the research on this topic. Therefore, we have constructed and published a Japanese lexical simplification system (SNOW S3) and a dataset for evaluation of the system (SNOW E4). These resources are available at the following URL:

http://www.jnlp.org/SNOW

2 Previous Work

Two datasets for evaluation of English lexical simplification have been published. Both were constructed by transforming a lexical substitution dataset, which was constructed in an English lexical substitution task of SemEval-2007 workshop (McCarthy and Navigli, 2007).

2.1 McCarthy Substitution Dataset

The English lexical substitution task of SemEval-2007 requires that the system finds words or phrases that one can substitute for the given target word in the given content. These target words are content words, and their details are shown in Table 1. These contexts are selected from the English Internet Corpus, which is a balanced and web-based corpus of English (Sharoff, 2006). This dataset consists of 2,010 sentences, 201 target words each with 10 sentences as contexts. Five annotators who are native English speakers proposed at most three appropriate substitutions for each of the target words within their contexts. When an appropriate paraphrasable word did not occur, the annotator propose paraphrasable phrases.

An example from this dataset is provided below. As a paraphrase of the adjective "bright" in this context, three annotators proposed "intelligent", another three annotators proposed "clever", and one annotator proposed "smart".

Context: During the siege, G. Robertson had ap-

[1] http://www.cs.pomona.edu/~dkauchak/simplification/
[2] https://www.ukp.tu-darmstadt.de/data/
[3] http://www.cs.york.ac.uk/semeval-2012/task1/
[4] http://people.cs.kuleuven.be/~jan.debelder/lseval.zip

Proceedings of the ACL-IJCNLP 2015 Student Research Workshop, pages 35–40,
Beijing, China, July 28, 2015.

Dataset	Sentence	Noun(%)	Verb(%)	Adjective(%)	Adverb(%)
McCarthy / Specia	2,010	580 (28.9)	520 (25.9)	560 (27.9)	350 (17.4)
De Belder	430	100 (23.3)	60 (14.0)	160 (37.2)	110 (25.6)
Ours (SNOW E4)	2,330	630 (27.0)	720 (30.9)	500 (21.5)	480 (20.6)

Table 1: Size of the dataset

pointed Shuja-ul-Mulk, who was a bright boy only 12 years old and the youngest surviving son of Aman-ul-Mulk, as the ruler of Chitral.

Gold-Standard: intelligent 3; clever 3; smart 1;

2.2 Specia Simplification Dataset

The English lexical simplification task of SemEval-2012 requires that the system ranks the target word and its several paraphrases according to how *simple* they are in the context. *Simple* means that the word is easy to understand for many people, including children and non-natives.

This dataset was annotated by fluent but non-native English speakers (college freshmen). The Trial dataset used four annotators, and the Test dataset used five annotators. These annotators ranked target words and their several paraphrases according to how simple they were in contexts from the lexical substitution dataset described in Section 2.1. Next, the ranks received from each annotator were integrated into the dataset. Finally, the gold-standard annotations were generated by averaging the annotations from all annotators.

An example from this dataset is provided below. When the following ranking was obtained from four annotators in a context, the ranks of "clear" were 1, 2, 1, 4, and the average rank was 2. Similarly, the average rank of each word calculated. Thus, the rank of "light" is 3.25, that of "bright" is 2.5, that of "luminous" is 4, and that of "well-lit" is 3.25. The final integrated ranking is obtained by rearranging the average ranks of these words in the ascending order, as shown below.

1: {clear}{light}{bright}{luminous}{well-lit}
2: {well-lit}{clear}{light}{bright}{luminous}
3: {clear}{bright}{light}{luminous}{well-lit}
4: {bright}{well-lit}{luminous}{clear}{light}
Gold: {clear}{bright}{light,well-lit}{luminous}

2.3 De Belder Simplification Dataset

De Belder and Moens (2012) also created a simplification dataset. They deleted enough simple target words included in the Basic English combined word list[5] from the lexical substitution dataset described in the Section 2.1 at first. As a result of deleting, the number of target words narrowed down from 201 to 43. Five annotators ranked these 43 target words and their several paraphrases according to how simple they were in the context.

These annotators were recruited using the Amazon Mechanical Turk[6]. De Belder and Moens requested annotators who were located in the U.S. and had completed at least 95% of their previous assignments correctly.

In the end, the rank from each annotator was integrated into the dataset. In this dataset, the noisy channel model was used in order to take account of the rank and reliability of each annotator.

3 Constructing Japanese Lexical Substitution Dataset

We have constructed a dataset for evaluation of Japanese lexical simplification. First, a Japanese lexical substitution dataset was constructed using the same method as McCarthy and Navigli (2007).

3.1 Selecting Target Words

We define target words as the list of content words (nouns, verbs, adjectives, and adverbs) that are common to two Japanese word dictionaries (IPADIC-2.7.0[7] and JUMANDIC-7.0[8]) in order to select the standard target words at first. Next, the following words were deleted from these words.

- Words that are already simple enough
- Words that have no substitutions
- Words that are a part of a compound word
- Words that are a part of an idiomatic phrase
- Low frequency words

We define simple words as words in Basic Vocabulary to Learn (Kai and Matsukawa, 2002), which is a receptive vocabulary for elementary school students. Words that are not registered

[5]http://simple.wikipedia.org/wiki/Wikipedia:Basic_English_combined_wordlist
[6]https://www.mturk.com
[7]http://sourceforge.jp/projects/ipadic/releases/24435/
[8]http://nlp.ist.i.kyoto-u.ac.jp/index.php?JUMAN

$$\frac{\sum_{p_1,p_2 \in P} \frac{p_1 \cap p_2}{p_1 \cup p_2}}{|P|} \quad (1)$$

$$\frac{\sum_j (rank_i(w_j) - \overline{rank_i})(rank_{ave}(w_j) - \overline{rank_{ave}})}{\sqrt{\sum_j (rank_i(w_j) - \overline{rank_i})^2 \sum_j (rank_{ave}(w_j) - \overline{rank_{ave}})^2}} \quad (2)$$

in SNOW D2 (Yamamoto and Yoshikura, 2013) are defined as words that have no substitutions. Low frequency words are defined as words that occurred less than 10 times over the 15 years in Japanese newspapers[9].

In the end, 250 words (nouns and verbs 75 each, adjectives and adverbs 50 each) were chosen as a target words at random.

3.2 Providing Paraphrases

An annotator provided several paraphrases for each target word in 10 contexts. These contexts were randomly selected from newspaper article. When providing a paraphrase, an annotator could refer to a dictionary but was not supposed to ask the other annotators for an opinion. When an annotator could not think of a paraphrase, they were permitted to supply no entry.

Five annotators for every fifty sentences were recruited using crowdsourcing service[10]. On average, each of these annotators contributed 5.38 paraphrases.

3.3 Merging All Annotations

Each annotator's result was evaluated, and all the results were merged into one dataset. Five new annotators for every fifty sentences were recruited through the crowdsourcing service. We adopted the paraphrases that more than three annotators rated appropriate by answering the question, "Is this paraphrase appropriate?" in the affirmative. When an annotator rated a paraphrase as inappropriate, they were shown the following two criteria.

1. A paraphrase is inappropriate if the sentence becomes unnatural as a result of the substitution of this paraphrase for the target word.
2. A paraphrase is inappropriate if the meaning of the sentence changes as a result of the substitution of this paraphrase for the target word.

An average of 4.50 lexical paraphrases were accepted. However, 170 sentences (17 target words) that all paraphrases have been evaluated to be inappropriate were discarded.

[9]http://www.nikkeibookvideo.com/kijidb/

[10]http://www.lancers.jp

Since we have sets of paraphrases for each target word and annotator, pairwise agreement was calculated between each pair of sets ($p_1, p_2 \in P$) from each possible pairing (P) according to the Equation (1), following previous research (McCarthy and Navigli, 2007). Inter-annotator agreement is 66.4%.

An English translation of an example from the dataset is provided below. As a paraphrase of the noun "appeal" in this context, one annotator proposed "advocate", another annotator proposed "exert", and three annotators proposed "promote".

Context: You can appeal for proud batting power.
Gold-Standard: advocate 1; promote 3; exert 1;

4 Transforming into Lexical Simplification Dataset

4.1 Ranking Paraphrases

These target words and their several paraphrases were ranked according to how simple they were in the context from the dataset that we built (as discussed in Section 3) in order to transform it into a dataset for evaluation of lexical simplification. The same annotators as those mentioned in section 3.3 worked on this task.

Finally, the total number of annotators is 500. Some 250 annotators provided paraphrases, others evaluated and ranked these paraphrases.

Inter-annotator agreement was calculated by Spearman's rank correlation coefficient, following previous research (Belder and Moens, 2012). Spearman's rank correlation coefficient is defined as in the Equation (2), where $\overline{rank_i}$ is the average rank of the words given by annotator i. To extend this equation to one annotator versus other annotators, we define the rank assigned by the $rank_{ave}$ to be the average of the ranks given by the other annotators. This agreement is 33.2%[11].

4.2 Merging All Rankings

All annotators' work results were merged into one dataset. The rank of each word was decided based

[11]While this score is apparently low, the highly subjective nature of the annotation task must be taken into account (Specia et al., 2012).

	all	%	noun	%	verb	%	adj	%	adv	%
1. # context pairs	10,485	-	2,835	-	3,240	-	2,250	-	2,160	-
2. # 1. with same list	1,593	15	789	28	348	11	168	7	288	13
3. # 2. with different rankings	948	60	344	44	262	75	129	77	213	74
4. # 3. with different top word	463	49	214	62	130	50	51	40	68	32

Table 2: Context dependency ratio

on the average of the rank from each annotator, following the previous research (Specia et al., 2012). The same rank is assigned to words that have the same average. In this study, the same annotator performed both the evaluation of paraphrases and their ranking. Therefore, any word that an annotator judged as an inappropriate paraphrase was not ranked. The minimum rank is assigned to these words that were not ranked at the time of the calculation of the average rank.

An English translation of an example from the dataset is provided below. When the following ranking was obtained from five annotators in a context, the ranks of "appeal" were 1, 2, 4, 2, 2, and the average rank was 2.2. Similarly, the average rank of "promote" is 2.2, that of "advocate" is 2.6, and that of "exert" is 3. The final integrated ranking is obtained by rearranging the average ranks of these words in the ascending order.

1: {appeal}{promote}{advocate}{exert}
2: {advocate}{appeal}{promote}{exert}
3: {promote}{exert}{advocate} #appeal
4: {exert}{appeal}{advocate}{promote}
5: {promote}{appeal}{advocate} #exert
Gold: {appeal, promote}{advocate}{exert}

4.3 Properties of the dataset

In 1,616 (69.4%) of the sentences, a target word can be replaced by one or more simpler words. In 420 (18.0%) of the cases, there is also one or more words that are equally complex. In 1,945 (83.5%) of the cases, there are words that are more complex. The average number of substitutions is 5.50. The average number of levels of difficulty is 4.94.

Table 2 shows how the relative simplicity of the target words and their paraphrases is context dependent. Only 15.2% of all context-pairs which share the target word have the same list of paraphrases. This shows that the meaning of many target words changed slightly in different contexts. In addition, 59.5% of combinations with the same list of paraphrases have different ranks of difficulty. This shows that the difficulty of a word

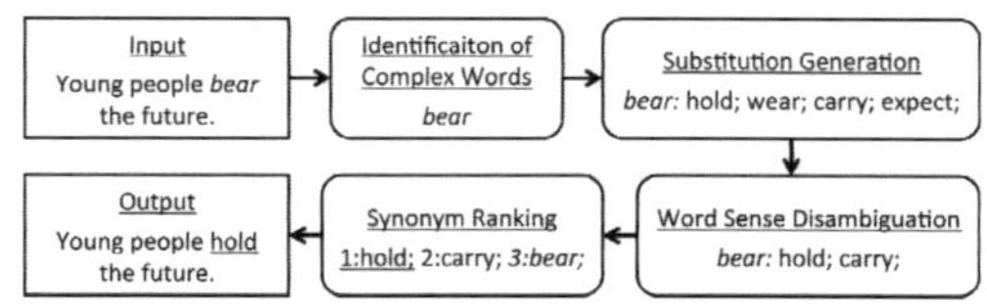

Figure 1: Outline of lexical simplification system

also changes slightly in different contexts. Among these, 48.8% is even different in the simplest word.

5 Constructing Japanese Lexical Simplification System

We have also constructed a lexical simplification system using four typical mechanisms of lexical simplification (Shardlow, 2014) shown in Figure1. We expect the standard system to be used as a baseline of Japanese lexical simplification. We also expect that the system can support the reading comprehension of a wide range of readers.

5.1 Identification of Complex Words

An input sentence is first analyzed by the Japanese morphological analyzers MeCab-0.993 (Kudo et al., 2004)[12] and IPADIC-2.7.0, and content words that are not included in the list of simple words are extracted as complex words. These complex words are not part of a compound word or an idiomatic phrase.

In this study, simple words are defined as the Basic Vocabulary to Learn; compound words are defined as the lists of entries from Japanese Wikipedia[13] and the Compound Verb Lexicon[14]; finally, idiomatic phrases are defined as the list of Japanese idiomatic phrases made by Sato (2007).

5.2 Substitution Generation

Several paraphrases are enumerated as candidates of a simple word for each complex word. These lexical paraphrases were selected from several Japanese lexical paraphrasing databases such as SNOW D2 (Yamamoto and Yoshikura, 2013),

[12]https://code.google.com/p/mecab/
[13]http://dumps.wikimedia.org/jawiki/
[14]http://vvlexicon.ninjal.ac.jp/

Precision	Recall	F-measure
0.89	0.08	0.15

Table 3: Performance of the system

Noun	Verb	Adjective	Adverb
62	65	3	0

Table 4: POS of the simplified target words

Japanese WordNet Synonyms Database[15], Verb Entailment Database[16], and Case Base for Basic Semantic Relations[16], following previous research (Kajiwara and Yamamoto, 2014).

5.3 Word Sense Disambiguation

If, given the context of the sentence, the list of suggested paraphrases for a complex word contains words that are improper in this context, these improper paraphrases are removed from the list. An input sentence receives a predicate-argument structure analysis using the Japanese predicate-argument structure analyzer SynCha-0.3 (Iida and Poesio, 2011)[17], and the predicate (verb or adjective), the arguments (nouns) and grammatical relations (case makers such as "*ga* (subject)", "*o* (object)", "*ni* (indirect object)") are extracted as a set of the form {predicate, relation, argument}.

Either the predicate or one of the arguments is identified as a complex word. A list is of candidate substitutions is generated for that word, followed by a list of sets of the form {predicate, relation, argument}, where the candidate substitutions are used instead of the complex word (so there will be as many of these sets as there are candidate substitutions). These new sets are checked against the Kyoto University Case Frame[18]. If the set is found there, the candidate substitution counts as a legitimate substitution; if the set is not found, the candidate substitution is not counted as a legitimate substitution. Kyoto University Case Frame is the list of predicate and argument pairs that have a case relationship, and it is built automatically (Kawahara and Kurohashi, 2006) from Web texts.

5.4 Synonym Ranking

All candidate words are given a degree of difficulty. The simplest word is used to replace the complex word in the input sentence, and the output sentence is generated.

In this study, Lexical Properties of Japanese (Amano and Kondo, 2000) is used for determining the degree of difficulty.

[15]http://nlpwww.nict.go.jp/wn-ja/jpn/downloads.html
[16]https://alaginrc.nict.go.jp/resources/nict-resource/
[17]http://www.cl.cs.titech.ac.jp/ ryu-i/syncha/
[18]http://www.gsk.or.jp/catalog/gsk2008-b/

5.5 Evaluation of the System by the Dataset

The performance of the lexical simplification system that was discussed in this section is estimated using the evaluation dataset that was constructed as discussed in Section 4. The performance of the system is shown in Table 3. In 146 sentences, the system converted a target word into another word; in 130 sentences, that output word was simpler than the target word defined by the evaluation dataset appropriately. In addition, the system converted 652 words in total, but only 146 words of these were the target words.

The details as to the parts of speech of the target words that got simplified appropriately are shown in Table 4. The system simplifies only the predicates and arguments extracted by the predicate-argument structure analysis. However, adverbs are not simplified since they are included in neither predicates nor arguments. In addition, an adjective may become a predicate, but it may also become part of a noun phrase by modifying a noun. The system simplifies only predicate adjectives.

An English translation of an example of several system outputs is provided below.

- It is {distributed –> dealt} to a {caller –> visitor} from foreign countries.
- {Principal –> President} Takagi of the bank presented an idea.

6 Final Remarks

We built a Japanese lexical simplification system and a dataset for evaluation of Japanese lexical simplification. Subsequently, we have published these resources on the Web.

The system can support the reading comprehension of a wide range of readers, including children and language learners. Since we have developed a standard system, we expect the system to be used as a baseline system of lexical simplification.

Furthermore, the dataset enables us to figure out system performance. This solves the problems of cost and reproducibility associated with the conventional manual evaluation and accelerates research on this topic.

References

Shigeaki Amano and Kimihisa Kondo. 2000. On the ntt psycholinguistic databases "lexical properties of japanese". *Journal of the Phonetic Society of Japan*, 4(2):44–50.

Jan De Belder and Marie-Francine Moens. 2010. Text simplification for children. *In Proceedings of the SIGIR Workshop on Accessible Search Systems*, pages 19–26.

Jan De Belder and Marie-Francine Moens. 2012. A dataset for the evaluation of lexical simplification. *In Proceedings of the 13th International Conference on Computational Linguistics and Intelligent Text Processing (CICLing-2012)*, pages 426–437.

Soojeong Eom, Markus Dickinson, and Rebecca Sachs. 2012. Sense-specific lexical information for reading assistance. *In Proceedings of the Seventh Workshop on Building Educational Applications Using NLP*, pages 316–325.

Colby Horn, Cathryn Manduca, and David Kauchak. 2014. Learning a lexical simplifier using wikipedia. *In Proceedings of the 52th Annual Meeting of the Associatioin for Computational Linguistics*, pages 458–463.

Ryu Iida and Massimo Poesio. 2011. A cross-lingual ilp solution to zero anaphora resolution. *The 49th Annual Meeting of the Association for Computational Linguistics: Human Language Technologies*, pages 804–813.

Mutsuro Kai and Toshihiro Matsukawa. 2002. *Method of Vocabulary Teaching: Vocabulary Table version*. Mitsumura Tosho Publishing Co., Ltd.

Tomoyuki Kajiwara and Kazuhide Yamamoto. 2014. Qualitative evaluation of available japanese resources for lexical paraphrasing. *IEICE Technical Report, NLC2014-37*, 114(366):43–48.

Tomoyuki Kajiwara, Hiroshi Matsumoto, and Kazuhide Yamamoto. 2013. Selecting proper lexical paraphrase for children. *In Proceedings of the 25th Conference on Computational Linguistics and Speech Processing*, pages 59–73.

David Kauchak. 2013. Improving text simplification language modeling using unsimplified text data. *In Proceedings of the 51th Annual Meeting of the Associatioin for Computational Linguistics*, pages 1537–1546.

Daisuke Kawahara and Sadao Kurohashi. 2006. A fully-lexicalized probabilistic model for japanese syntactic and case structure analysis. *In Proceedings of the Human Language Technology Conference of the North American Chapter of the Association for Computational Linguistics*, pages 176–183.

Taku Kudo, Kaoru Yamamoto, and Yuji Matsumoto. 2004. Applying conditional random fields to japanese morphological analysis. *Proceedings of the Conference on Empirical Methods in Natural Language Processing*, pages 230–237.

Diana McCarthy and Roberto Navigli. 2007. Semeval-2007 task10: English lexical substitution task. *In Proceedings of the 4th International Workshop on Semantic Evaluations (SemEval-2007)*, pages 48–53.

Manami Moku, Kazuhide Yamamoto, and Ai Makabi. 2012. Automatic easy japanese translation for information accessibility of foreigners. *In Proceedings of the Workshop on Speech and Language Processing Tools in Education*, pages 85–90.

Satoshi Sato. 2007. Compilation of a comparative list of basic japanese idioms from five sources. *The Special Interest Group Technical Reports of IPSJ, 2007-NL-178*, pages 1–6.

Matthew Shardlow. 2014. A survey of automated text simplification. *International Journal of Advanced Computer Science and Applications, Special Issue on Natural Language Processing*, pages 58–70.

Serge Sharoff. 2006. Open-source corpora: Using the net to fish for linguistic data. *International Journal of Corpus Linguistics, 11(4)*, pages 435–462.

Lucia Specia, Sujay Kumar Jauhar, and Rada Mihalcea. 2012. Semeval-2012 task 1: English lexical simplification. *In Proceedings of the 6th International Workshop on Semantic Evaluation (SemEval-2012)*, pages 347–355.

Kazuhide Yamamoto and Kotaro Yoshikura. 2013. Manual construction of lexical paraphrase dictionary of japanese verbs, adjectives, and adverbs. *In Proceedings of 19th Annual Meeting of Association for Natural Language Processing*, pages 276–279.

Zhemin Zhu, Delphine Bernhard, and Iryna Gurevych. 2010. A monolingual tree-based translation model for sentence simplification. *In Proceedings of the 23rd International Conference on Computational Linguistics*, pages 1353–1361.

Learning to Map Dependency Parses to Abstract Meaning Representations

Wei-Te Chen
Department of Computer Science
University of Colorado at Boulder
Weite.Chen@colorado.edu

Abstract

Abstract Meaning Representation (AMR) is a semantic representation language used to capture the meaning of English sentences. In this work, we propose an AMR parser based on dependency parse rewrite rules. This approach transfers dependency parses into AMRs by integrating the syntactic dependencies, semantic arguments, named entity and co-reference information. A dependency parse to AMR graph aligner is also introduced as a preliminary step for designing the parser.

1 Introduction

Abstract Meaning Representation (AMR) (Banarescu et al., 2013) is a semantic formalism that expresses the logical meanings of English sentences in the form of a directed, acyclic graph. AMR focuses on the semantic concepts (nodes on the graph), and relations (labeled edges on the graph) between those concepts. AMR relies heavily on predicate-argument structures defined in the PropBank (PB) (Palmer et al., 2005). The representation encodes rich information, including semantic roles, named entities, and co-reference information. Fig. 1 shows an example AMR.

```
(j / join-01
      :ARG0 (p / person
            :name (p2 / name :op1 "Pierre" :op2 "Vinken")
            :age (t / temporal-quantity :quant 61
                  :unit (y / year)))
      :ARG1 (b / board
            :ARG1-of (h / have-org-role-91
                  :ARG0 p
                  :ARG2 (d2 / director
                        :mod (e / executive :polarity -))))
      :time (d / date-entity :month 11 :day 29))
```

Figure 1: The AMR annotation of sentence "Pierre Vinken, 61 years old, will join the board as a nonexecutive director Nov. 29."

In this proposal, we focus on the design of an automatic AMR parser in a supervised fashion from dependency parses. In contrast with recent semantic parsing algorithms, we start the parsing process from the dependency parses rather than the sentences. A dependency parse provides both the semantic dependency information for the sentence, and the structure of the relations between the head word and their dependencies. These can provide strong features for semantic parsing. By using a binary-branching bottom-up shift-reduced algorithm, the statistical model for the rewrite rules can be learned discriminatively. Although the AMR parser is my thesis topic, in this proposal we will pay more attention to preliminary work - the AMR -Dependency Parse aligner.

To extract the rewrite rules and the statistical model, we need the links between AMR concepts and the word nodes within the dependency parse. An example alignment is shown in Fig. 2. Alignment between an AMR concept and dependency node is needed because 1) it represents the meaning of the sub-graph of the concept and its child concepts corresponding to the phrase of the head word node, and 2) the dependency node contains sufficient information for the extraction of rewrite rules. For example, the word node "Vinken" on the dependency parse side in Fig. 2 links to the lexical concept "Vinken" and, furthermore, links to the "*p2/name*" and the "*p/person*" concepts since "Vinken" is the head of the named entity (NE) "Pierre Vinken" and the head of the noun phrase "Pierre Vinken, 61 years old." The secondary aim of this proposal is to design an alignment model between AMR concepts and dependency parses. We use EM to search the hidden derivations by combining the features of lexical form, relation label, NE, semantic role, etc. After EM processing, both the alignments and all the feature probabilities can be estimated.

The design of a rewrite-based AMR parser is described in Sec. 2, and the aligner is in Sec. 3. Our preliminary experiments and results are pre-

Proceedings of the ACL-IJCNLP 2015 Student Research Workshop, pages 41–46,
Beijing, China, July 28, 2015.

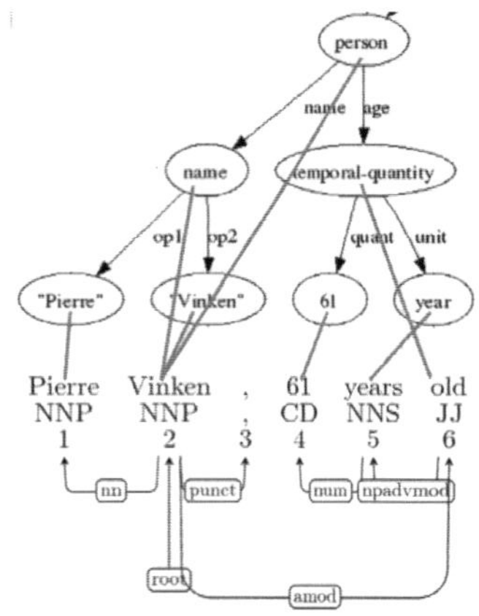

Figure 2: The alignment between an AMR subgraph and a dependency parse. A red line links the corresponding concept and dependency node.

sented in Sec. 4, followed by future work.

2 Rewrite Based AMR Parser

AMR is a rooted, directed, acyclic graph. For example, the concept **join-01** in Fig. 1 is the root meaning of the sentence, which links to the child concepts **Arg0**, **Arg1**, and **time**. AMR adheres to the following principles (Banarescu et al., 2013):

- AMRs are rooted acyclic graphs with labels (relations) on edges. These labels indicate the directed relation between two concepts.
- AMRs abstract away from syntactic idiosyncracies of a language, and instead attempt to capture only the core meaning of a sentence.
- AMRs use the PB framesets as relation labels (Palmer et al., 2005). For example, the relation labels (i.e., ARG0, ARG1) of "join-01" concept in Fig. 1 correspond to the roles of the PB frame "join-v."
- AMRs combine multiple layers of linguistic annotation, like coreference, NE, semantic role, etc., in a single structure.

The above basic characteristics make the parsing of AMRs a difficult task. First, because AMR abstracts away from syntactic idiosyncrasies, we need a model to link the AMR concepts to words in the original sentence, in order to obtain external lexical, syntactic and semantic features. Secondly, the parser should learn the different feature transformation probabilities jointly since AMRs combine several linguistic annotations. Moreover,

(x)/NP → :op(x)	-$r1$
(x) nn (y) → :name (name(x, y))	-$r2$
(x)/CD → :quant(x)	-$r3$
(x)/NNS → :unit(x)	-$r4$
npadvmod $(x)(y)$ → temporal-quanity(x, y)	-$r5$
old/JJ (x) → :age(x)	-$r6$
NE_PERSON$(x)(y)$ → person(x, y)	-$r7$

Table 1: Sample Rewrite Rules

AMR uses graph variables and reentrancy to express coreference (e.g., "p" variable in Fig 1 appears twice – in *:ARG0* of *join-01* and *:ARG0* of *have-org-role-91*). The reentrancy prevents the AMR graph from begin a tree structure. During parsing decoding, a polynomial time algorithm should be replaced by alternative algorithms, like beam search, to avoid an exponential running time.

JAMR (Flanigan et al., 2014) is the first system for AMR parsing, which identifies the concepts, and then searches for a maximum spanning connected subgraph (MSCG) on a fully connected graph to identify the relations between concepts. The search algorithm is similar to the maximum spanning tree algorithms. To assure the final connected graph conforms to linguistic constraints, JAMR uses Lagrangian relaxation (Geoffrion, 2010) to supplement the MSCG algorithm. JAMR reaches a 58% Smatch score (Cai and Knight, 2013) on automatic concept and relation identification data, and 80% on gold concept and automatic relation identification data.

2.1 Our Shift-Reduce Rewrite Rule Parser

Rewrite rule based parser is a bottom-up converter from dependency parses to AMRs. The process starts from the leaf word node on the dependency parse. By applying rewrite-rules to each word node, we obtain and assemble the sub-graphs of our target AMR. Sample rewrite rules are listed in Table 1. In these rules, the left hand side contains the dependency information (e.g. word lemma, POS, relation label, NE tag, etc). The right hand side is the AMR concept and its template for filling variables from previous parsing steps. The sample derivation steps are listed in Table 2. For every step, it shows the derivation rule applied (in Table 1), and the concept name, $c1$-$c8$.

This approach to parsing could be implemented with a shift-reduce algorithm (Wang et al., 2015). We define a stack and a list of tokens, which stores the dependency words in the order of tree traversal. Several actions are defined to operate on the list(L) and the stack(S):

Derivation	Apply Rule	Concept Name
Pierre/NNP → :op Pierre	$r1$	$c1$
Vinken/NNP → :op Vinken	$r1$	$c2$
$(c1)$ nn $(c2)$ → :name (name :op1 Pierre :op2 Vinekn)	$r2$	$c3$
61/CD → :quant 61	$r3$	$c4$
years/NNS → :unit year	$r4$	$c5$
npadvmod $(c4)(c5)$ → temporal-quanity :quant 61 :unit year	$r5$	$c6$
old/JJ $(c6)$ → :age (temporal-quanity :quant 61 :unit year)	$r6$	$c7$
NE_PERSON $(c3)(c7)$ → person :name (name :op1 Pierre :op2 Vinekn) :age (temporal-quanity :quant 61 :unit year)	$r7$	$c8$

Table 2: The derivation for parsing "Pierre Vinken, 61 years old" from dep. parse to AMR

- **Shift** Remove the dependency word from L, apply the rules, and push the new concept to S.
- **Reduce** Move the two top sub-concepts from S, apply the rules, and push it back to S.
- **Unary** Move the top sub-concept from S, apply the rules, and push it back to S.
- **Finish** If no more dependency words are in the list, and one concept is in S, then return.

The final AMR concept would be stored at the top of the stack. It is guaranteed that all the AMR expressions can be derived from the dependency parses by using the shift-reduce algorithm.

3 Dependency Parses to AMR Aligner

A preliminary step for our rewrite-based parser is the alignment between the AMR and the dependency parse. JAMR (Flanigan et al., 2014) provides a heuristic aligner between an AMR concept and the word or phrase of a sentence. They use a set of aligner rules, like NE, fuzzy NE, data entity, etc., with a greedy strategy to match the alignments. This aligner achieves a 90% F_1 score on hand aligned AMR-sentence pairs. On the other hand, Pourdamghani et al. (2014) present a generative model to align from AMR graphs to sentence strings. They raises concerns about the lack of sufficient data for learning derivation rules. Instead, they propose a string-to-string alignment model, which transfers the AMR expression to a linearized string representation. Then they use several IBM word alignment models (Brown et al., 1993) on this task. IBM Model-4 with a symmetric method reaches the highest F_1 score of 83.1%. Separately analyzing the alignments of roles and non-roles (lexical leaf on AMR), the F_1 scores are 49.3% and 89.8%, respectively.

In comparison to previous work, our aligner estimates the alignments by learning the transformation probability of lexical form, relations, named entities and semantic roles features jointly. Both the alignment and transformation probabilities are initialized for the training of parser.

3.1 Our Aligner Model with EM Algorithm

Our approach, based on the existing IBM Model (Brown et al., 1993), is an AMR-to-Dependency parse aligner, which represents one AMR as a list of Concepts $C = \langle c_1, c_2, \ldots, c_{|C|} \rangle$, and the corresponding dependency parse as a list of dependency word nodes $D = \langle d_1, d_2, \ldots, d_{|D|} \rangle$. The alignment A is a set of mapping functions a, which link Concept c_j to dependency word node d_i, $a : c_j \rightarrow d_i$. Our model adopts an asymmetric EM approach, instead of the standard symmetric one. We can always find the dependency label path between any pair of dependency word nodes. However, the number of concept relation label paths is not deterministic. Thus, we select the alignment direction of AMR to dependency parse only, and one-to-one mapping, in our model.

The objective function is to learn the parameter θ in the AMR-to-Dependency Parse of EM:

$$\theta = \operatorname{argmax} L_\theta(AMR|DEP)$$

$$L_\theta(AMR|DEP) = \sum_{k=1}^{|S|} \sum_{A} P(C^{(k)}, A|D^{(k)}; t, q)$$

where L_θ is the likelihood that we would like to maximize, S is the training data set. We will explain the transformation probability t and the alignment probability q below.

Expectation-Step

The E-Step estimates the likelihood of the input AMR and dependency parse by giving the transformation probability t and alignment probability q. The likelihood can be calculated using:

$$P(A|C, D) = \prod_{j=1}^{|C|} P(c_j|a(c_j))$$

$$P(c_j|d_i, |C|, |D|) = t(c_j|d_i) * q(d_i|c_j, |C|, |D|)$$

We would like to calculate all the probabilities of possible alignments A between c_j and d_i. The transformation probability t is a combination (multiple) probability of several different features:

- $P_{lemma}(c_j|d_i)$: the lemma probability is the probability of the concept name of c_j, conditioned on the dependency word of d_i.

- $P_{rel}(Label(c_j, c_j^p)|RelPath_{dep}(a(c_j), a(c_j^p)))$: the relation probability is the probability of the relation label between c_i and its parent concept c_i^p, given the relation path between the dependency word nodes $a(c_i)$ and $a(c_i^p)$. e.g., the relation probability of $c_j = 61$ and $a(c_j) = \underline{61}$ in Fig. 2 is $P(quant|\underline{npadvmod \downarrow num \downarrow})$.
- $P_{NE}(Name(c_j)|Type_{NE}(a(c_j)))$: the NE probability is the probability of the name of c_j, given the NE type (e.g., PERSON, DATE, ORG, etc.) contained by $a(c_j)$).
- $P_{SR}(Label(c_j, c_j^p)|Pred(a(c_j^p)), Arg(a(c_j)))$: the semantic role probability is the probability of relation label between c_j and its parent c_j^p, conditioned on the predicate word of $a(c_j^p)$ and argument type of $a(c_j)$ if $a(c_j)$ is semantic argument of predicate $a(c_j^p)$.

On the other hand, the alignment probability $q(Dist(a(c_j), a(c_j^p))|c_j, |C|, |D|)$ can be interpreted as the probability of the distance between $a(c_j)$ and $a(c_j^p)$ on dependency parse D, conditioned on c_j, the lengths of D and C.

Maximization-Step

In the M-Step, the parameter θ^r is updated from the previous round of θ^{r-1}, in order to maximize the likelihood $L_\theta(AMR|DEP)$:

$$t(C|D; AMR, DEP) = \frac{\sum_{(AMR,DEP)} cnt(C|D; AMR, DEP)}{\sum_C \sum_{(AMR,DEP)} cnt(C|D; AMR, DEP)}$$

$$q(D|C; AMR, DEP) = \frac{\sum_{(AMR,DEP)} cnt(D|C; AMR, DEP)}{\sum_D \sum_{(AMR,DEP)} cnt(D|C; AMR, DEP)}$$

where cnt is the normalized count that is collected from the accumulating probability of all possible alignment from the E-step. EM iterates the E-step and M-step until convergence.

Initialization

Before iterating, the transformation probability t and alignment probability q must be initialized. We use these steps to initialize the parameters:

1. Assign a fixed value, say 0.9, to $P_{lemma}(c_j|d_i)$ if the concept name of c_j is identical or a partial match to the dependency word node d_i. Otherwise, initialize it uniformly;
2. Run the EM algorithm with the initialized P_{lemma} only (Similar to IBM Model 1, which is only concerned with translation probability);
3. Initialize all the other parameters, i.e., P_{rel}, P_{NE}, P_{SR}, and q with the development data;
4. Run the completed EM algorithm with the P_{lemma} we obtained from Step 2 and other probabilities from Step 3.

The extra EM for the initialization of P_{lemma} is to estimate a more reasonable P_{lemma}, and to speed up the convergence of the second round of EM.

Decoding

To find the alignment of $\langle C, D \rangle$, we define the search for alignments as follows:

$$\begin{aligned} &\operatorname*{argmax}_A P(A|C, D) \\ &= \operatorname*{argmax}_A \prod_{j=1}^{|C|} t(c_j|a(c_j)) * q(a(c_j)|c_j, |C|, |D|) \end{aligned}$$

This decoding problem finds the alignment A with the maximum likelihood. A dynamic programming (DP) algorithm is designed to extract the target alignment without exhaustively searching all candidate alignments, which will take $O(|D|^{|C|})$.

This DP algorithm starts from the leaf concepts and then walks through parent concepts. In c_j, we need to produce the following likelihoods:

1. Accumulated likelihood for aligning to any d_i from all the child concepts of c_j
2. Likelihood of P_{lemma} and P_{NE}
3. Likelihood of P_{rel} and P_{SR} for parent concept c_j^p aligned to any dependency word node d_l.

In step (3), we need to find the d_l, aligned by c_j^p, that maximizes the likelihood. The accumulated likelihood is then stored in a list with size=$|D|$. We can trace back and find the most likely alignments in the end. The running time of this algorithm is $O(|C||D|^2)$. This algorithm does not include reentrancy cases. One solution to be explored in future work is to use a beam-search algorithm instead.

4 Preliminary Experiments and Results

Here, we describe a preliminary experiment for the AMR-Dependency Parse aligner, including the data description, experimental setup, and results.

4.1 Data

The LDC AMR release 1.0 consists of 13,051 AMR-English sentence pairs[1]. To match an AMR

[1]LDC AMR release 1.0, Release date: June 16, 2014 https://catalog.ldc.upenn.edu/LDC2014T12

Split	Sent.	Tokens	# of NE	# of Pred.	# of Args
Train	1,000	19,923	1,510	4,231	7,739
Dev.	100	2,328	239	235	526
Test	100	1,672	80	199	445

Table 3: The data split of train/dev./test set. "# of NE", "# of Pred." and "# of Args" stand for the number of named entities, predicate and argument annotations in the data set, respectively.

	P	R	F_1
P_{lemma}	56.7	50.5	53.4
Combination	61.1	53.4	57.0

Table 4: Experiment Results

with its corresponding dependency parse, we select the sentences which appear in the OntoNotes 5.0 release[2] as well, then randomly select 1,000 of them as our training set. The OntoNotes data contains TreeBank, PB, and NE annotations. Statistics about the AMR and OntoNotes corpus and the train/dev./test splits are given in Table 3. We manually align the AMR concepts and dependency word nodes in the dev. and test sets. We initialize P_{rel}, P_{NE}, and P_{SR} with the dev. set.

4.2 Results

We run our first round of EM (Step 2 in Initialization of Sec. 3.1) for 100 iterations, then use the second round (Step 4 in Initialization of Sec. 3.1) for another 100 iterations. We run our decoding algorithm and evaluation on the test set after the first and second round of EM. Due to time constraints, we did not train the q here.

The experimental results are listed in Table 4. We evaluate the performance on the precision, recall, and F_1 score. Using just the P_{lemma} (a similar approach to (Pourdamghani et al., 2014)), we achieve 53.4% F_1 score on the test set. On the other hand, our aligner reaches 57.0% F_1 score with the full aligner.

5 Conclusion and Future Work

In this research, we briefly introduce AMR. We describe the design principles and characteristics of AMR, and show how the AMR parser task is important, yet difficult. We present the basic idea for a proposed AMR parser, based on the shift-reduce algorithm. We also present an AMR-Dependency Parse aligner, because such an aligner will be a necessary first step before parsing. The alignment and the estimated feature probabilities are obtained by running the EM algorithm, which could be use directly for the AMR parser.

In the future, we will be following these steps to develop the proposed rewrite-based parser:

Implemention of our rewrite-based AMR parser: We would like to implement the proposed rewrite-based AMR parser. In comparison to the parser of Flanigan (2014) , we believe our parser could perform better on the runtime. We also plan to experiment with the data generated by an automatic dependency parser.

Expand the experimental data of aligner: One problem discovered in our preliminary experiments was that of data sparsity, especially for P_{lemma}. The LDC AMR Release contains 18,779 AMR/English sentences, and 8,996 of them are contained in the OntoNotes release as well. Therefore, increasing the training data size from the release is one solution to improve the performance of our aligner from the unsatisfactory results. Using external lexical resources, like WordNet, is another promising solution to extend to snyonyms.

Evaluation of the aligner with existing parser: Since our aligner provides the alignment between the dependency word node and both the AMR leaf concept and role concept, we assume that our aligner could improve not only our rewrite-based parser but other parsers as well. To verify this, we hope to submit our improved alignment results to a state-of-the-art AMR parser, and evaluate the parsing results.

Acknowledgments

We gratefully acknowledge the support of the National Science Foundation Grants IIS-1116782, A Bayesian Approach to Dynamic Lexical Resources for Flexible Language Processing, 0910992 IIS:RI: Richer Representations for Machine Translation, and NSF IIA-0530118 PIRE (a subcontract from Johns Hopkins) for the 2014 Frederick Jelinek Memorial Workshop for Meaning Representations in Language and Speech Processing, and funding under the BOLT and Machine Reading programs, HR0011-11-C-0145 (BOLT) FA8750-09-C-0179 (M.R.). Any opinions, findings, and conclusions or recommendations expressed in this material are those of the authors and do not necessarily reflect the views of the National Science Foundation.

[2]LDC OntoNotes Release 5.0, Release date: October 16, 2013 https://catalog.ldc.upenn.edu/LDC2013T19

References

Laura Banarescu, Claire Bonial, Shu Cai, Madalina Georgescu, Kira Griffitt, Ulf Hermjakob, Kevin Knight, Philipp Koehn, Martha Palmer, and Nathan Schneider. 2013. Abstract meaning representation for sembanking.

Peter F. Brown, Vincent J. Della Pietra, Stephen A. Della Pietra, and Robert L. Mercer. 1993. The mathematics of statistical machine translation: Parameter estimation. *Comput. Linguist.*, 19(2):263–311, June.

Shu Cai and Kevin Knight. 2013. Smatch: an evaluation metric for semantic feature structures. In *Proceedings of the 51st Annual Meeting of the Association for Computational Linguistics (Volume 2: Short Papers)*, pages 748–752. Association for Computational Linguistics.

J. Flanigan, S. Thomson, J. Carbonell, C. Dyer, and N. A. Smith. 2014. A discriminative graph-based parser for the abstract meaning representation. In *Proc. of ACL*, Baltimore, Maryland, June. Association for Computational Linguistics.

ArthurM. Geoffrion. 2010. Lagrangian relaxation for integer programming. In Michael Jnger, Thomas M. Liebling, Denis Naddef, George L. Nemhauser, William R. Pulleyblank, Gerhard Reinelt, Giovanni Rinaldi, and Laurence A. Wolsey, editors, *50 Years of Integer Programming 1958-2008*, pages 243–281. Springer Berlin Heidelberg.

Martha Palmer, Dan Guildea, and Paul Kingsbury. 2005. The Proposition Bank: An annotated corpus of semantic roles. *Computational Linguistics*, 31(1):71–105, March.

Nima Pourdamghani, Yang Gao, Ulf Hermjakob, and Kevin Knight. 2014. Aligning english strings with abstract meaning representation graphs. In *Proceedings of the 2014 Conference on Empirical Methods in Natural Language Processing (EMNLP)*, pages 425–429. Association for Computational Linguistics.

Chuan Wang, Xue Nianwen, and Pradhan Sameer. 2015. A transition-based algorithm for amr parsing. In *Proceedings of the 2015 Conference of the North American Chapter of the Association for Computational Linguistics: Human Language Technologies*. Association for Computational Linguistics.

Author Index

Association for Computational Linguistics
209 N. Eighth Street
Stroudsburg, Pennsylvania 18360

ISBN 978-1-5108-0848-5

CURRAN ASSOCIATES INC.
proceedings.com